THE
CLASSROOM TEACHER'S
INCLUSION
HANDBOOK

2nd Edition, Revised and Expanded

Other Books by Jerome C. Yanoff

The Classroom Teacher's Trouble-Shooting Handbook

The Excellent Teacher's Handbook

THE
CLASSROOM TEACHER'S
INCLUSION
HANDBOOK

Practical Methods for Integrating Students with Special Needs

JEROME C. YANOFF

2nd Edition, Revised and Expanded

arthur coyle press
chicago, illinois

The Classroom Teacher's Inclusion Handbook

Copyright 2000, 2007 by Jerome C. Yanoff

Arthur Coyle Press
P.O. Box 59435
Chicago, Illinois 60659-0435
www.arthurcoylepress.com

Edited by Mary Edsey.

Printed in the U.S.A.
First printing 2000.
Second printing 2001.
Third printing 2002.
Fourth printing 2007, completely revised.

10 9 8 7 6 5

Publisher's Cataloging in Publication Data

Yanoff, Jerome C.
The Classroom Teacher's Inclusion Handbook / Jerome C. Yanoff
Includes 225 pages and index.
ISBN 0-9665947-5-4

1. Teachers
2. Inclusion
3. Special Education

371.9   99-093375

Contents

Introduction

During much of our nation's history the special needs of children who could not function in a regular classroom were largely ignored. There were no special programs for them. Schools discouraged them from attending or expelled them if they presented a hardship.

In the mid-1800s through the efforts of such people as Thomas Hopkins Gallaudet and Alexander Graham Bell, some programs, most notably for the deaf, were established to teach children with special needs. By the turn of the century scattered programs served the special needs of only a small percentage of these children, but in the years following World War II about half were in special programs.

The first special education programs functioned apart from the regular classrooms, often in separate buildings. Teachers who worked with these children were called "special education teachers." Each teacher was trained in one area of special education, such as teaching the deaf or teaching the blind. The children were placed in or removed from their programs as administrators saw fit. Often the education of the child was not their primary concern.

The current philosophy that all children, even those with special needs, have a right to an education grew out of the Civil Rights movement of the 1960s. Families who had children with disabilities realized that their children too were being denied a basic American right—that of a free public education.

In 1975 President Gerald Ford signed Public Law 94-142, the Education for All Handicapped Children Act. Its most important provision insured that all children would be presented with a free and appropriate education in the least restrictive environment. The rights of special needs students were expanded under subsequent laws, particularly 99-457 and 101-476 entitled the Individuals with Disabilities Education Act or IDEA. They increased the amount of time and types of services students with special needs were able to obtain.

By the 1980s many parents and educators believed that students with special needs would learn better with their neighborhood friends in regular classrooms than in special classrooms with students who all had the same disability. To accommodate this new idea several states mandated that new teachers become acquainted with techniques for working with all types of special needs students. However, the required training (usually one survey course) provides only enough information to begin working with such students.

The Classroom Teacher's Inclusion Handbook continues that education with detailed information about each type of special need and practical suggestions for working with students who have them. The ideas in this book come from the author's 40 years of personal experience in the field of special education (27 years as a high school special education teacher and 13 years as a college teacher of special education survey courses), as well as observing and working with others.

About the Author

Author Jerome C. Yanoff taught special education in public school classrooms from 1966 to 1993. During that time he served ten years as the union representative in his high school and six years on the executive board of the Chicago Teachers Union as a high school vice president. He has been elected several times as a delegate to the Illinois Federation of Teachers and the American Federation of Teachers. He has been teaching in the Special Education Department of National-Louis University in Chicago since 1994 and has been an active lecturer and workshop leader in the fields of Special Education and Behavior Management since 2000.

Mr. Yanoff can be reached through Best Practice Training and Consulting Services, P.O. Box 180018, Chicago, IL 60618 or 773 -728-7416.

How to Use This Book

The *Classroom Teacher's Inclusion Handbook* is an easy-to-follow book written for the regular classroom teacher. The first chapter includes an overview of inclusion and general information about students with special needs. The fourteen chapters that follow are categorized by the specific mental or physical disabilities or exceptionalities of students. Some chapters are then subdivided to more specific types.

Each chapter or section begins with a definition of the disability or exceptionality. Most definitions listed are from Public Law 94-142 or its updates. Named the Individuals with Disabilities Education Act (IDEA) in 1990, the law was first passed by the federal government in 1975 and has been amended several times since—most recently in 1997. This landmark legislation mandated special education in all public schools. It is the principle source for educators to define students with special needs. Other sources of definitions are used in some chapters in which a more concise definition was available.

Following the definitions, each chapter then lists by bulletpoint important facts, characteristics, and suggestions for working with students with each type of special need. Because each disability or exceptionality presents unique problems, other topics, such as characteristics of undiagnosed problems, are also included when appropriate. Please note that in all sections, students who possess the problem being discussed may exhibit only one or several of the characteristics listed. This is followed by a glossary of words likely to be used by professionals when discussing these students. To help the reader acquire further information, each chapter concludes with a list of reference books and Web sites.

In an unusual situation the classroom teacher may receive special instructions from a doctor, school nurse, special education teacher or parent concerning an individual student that oppose the suggestions in this book. If such a situation should occur, follow the specific instructions given and not the suggestion in this book.

While using this book and learning more about students with special needs, it will become apparent that students with special needs are different from regular students. The differences may be very small or considerable. Keep in mind that it is all right to be different, in fact, it is differences which make us interesting, Knowing this will have you on the road to enjoying all your students—no matter what their differences may be.

Six Essential Elements for Successful Inclusion

1. The district sees inclusion as a program to serve children.
2. The principal sees inclusion as a way to better education.
3. The parents see inclusion as an opportunity for their child.
4. The teacher sees inclusion as a challenge and a way to attain personal growth.
5. The classmates see inclusion as a chance for personal development.
6. The student with special needs sees inclusion as an entrance to a more normal life.

Six Harmful Attitudes That Can Ruin Inclusion

1. The district sees inclusion as an opportunity to save money.
2. The principal sees inclusion as a way to save space in the school and to punish teachers in disfavor.
3. The parents see inclusion as a way to confirm denial of their child's problems.
4. The teacher sees inclusion as an imposition and deviation from comfortable routine.
5. The classmates see inclusion as an opportunity to ridicule.
6. The special needs student sees inclusion as an environment of exposure and shame.

Chapter I

Inclusion

Definition

Inclusion is the practice of placing students with special needs in the regular classroom with non-disabled students and providing specialized services and/or specialized curriculum for them.

The philosophy of inclusion is twofold: (1) children with special needs will develop better socially if they can attend classes with non-disabled children; and (2) children who are non-disabled will become more knowledgeable and sensitive when working with children who have disabilities.

Important Facts about Inclusion

- Though the terms "inclusion" and "mainstreaming" are sometimes used interchangeably, mainstreaming differs in that the students with special needs placed in the regular classroom in this program receive the same education and services the other students are receiving.

- The procedure for placing a student in a special education program is regulated by federal law. When it becomes apparent that a student with disabilities cannot function in the regular classroom without receiving special education services, the parents, teacher, or administrator, who feels the student requires special education services, initiates a multi-disciplinary conference called a "staffing." Prior to the conference the student is tested in appropriate areas. At the staffing, parents and other adults involved with the student's education determine whether the student needs special education services. If so, a plan, known as the Individual Education Plan (IEP), is made to provide the assistance the student needs. The IEP is an agreement between the school and the parents listing the services the school will provide to the child. The IEP must include the following:

  1. the present educational abilities of the student,
  2. the long range goals for the school year,
  3. the short range goals necessary for reaching the long range goals,
  4. the specific educational support services to be provided by the school,
  5. the extent, if any, of mainstream or inclusion participation, and

2

6. a method of recording progress toward achieving the goals and objectives.

• In addition to the academic program the following services may also be offered: *(a)* audiology, *(b)* counseling, *(c)* medical services for further diagnoses and evaluation, *(d)* occupational therapy, *(e)* parent counseling and training, *(f)* physical therapy, *(g)* psychological services, *(h)* recreation, *(i)* rehabilitation counseling, *(j)* school health services, *(k)* social work services, *(l)* speech pathology, and *(m)* transportation. Often the school boards are reluctant to offer these services unless they absolutely have to, as each one is an additional expense to be borne by the local district.

• The amount of extra work required of a regular classroom teacher with a student with special needs depends on the school regulations, the union contract and the willingness and abilities of the teacher. A student with special needs who is appropriate for inclusion should fit into the class with minimal procedural alteration. Extra meetings, specialized training and special curriculum should be the responsibility of the special education teacher, not the regular classroom teacher. Additional paperwork, however, must be recorded by the classroom teacher— special reports and anecdotal material; changes in the student's medication; and additional record keeping, if the school employs a behavior modification program.

• The student should be one of the participants at the writing of the IEPs. He should be aware of the special education services he will receive and how they will help him.

• Most disabilities do not affect what a student learns but how a student learns.

• The classroom teacher cannot and should not be expected to be a specialist in each area of special education nor should the parents or administrators demand it.

• Inclusion works better when the professionals in the school collaborate. However, not all professionals are available or are willing to collaborate. The regular classroom teacher must be prepared to continue teaching their student with special needs with or without collaboration.

• If the classroom teacher feels good about inclusion, the student with special needs will thrive. If the teacher feels resentful about the extra work, the student will likely suffer.

- The receiving classroom teacher should remember she is modeling behavior for the entire class. If she shows she is unaccepting of the student with special needs, the other students won't accept him either.

- Sometimes, when a school adopts a policy of inclusion, the special education teacher is adverse to it. This may be because they are having difficulty letting go of their students or they may feel a loss of importance in the school.

- Some students with special needs may be assigned an aid. The teacher is still in charge of the class and responsible for the student with the special needs, even if the aid is older and more experienced working with children. The teacher and aid should respect each other's expertise and work together.

- The number of special education students placed in one classroom depends on the type of disability each student has and the willingness of the teacher—there could be six special education students who require a little additional help or one who is a constant handful.

- Though a regular classroom teacher cannot refuse to accept a student with special needs the teacher may be able to refuse to perform certain services which are inappropriate for a teacher to do, such as some medical procedures, toileting, lifting, feeding, etc. The teacher should refer to her contract on this issue.

- It is unlikely a classroom teacher would be sued if something goes wrong, if for no other reason than most teachers do not have enough money to make a legal suit worthwhile. It is more likely that a school board or school district would be sued.

- The number of students with special education needs is increasing because *(a)* medical advances are saving the lives of children born prematurely, of children with serious birth defects, and of children affected by disease or serious accidents; *(b)* parents are responding to the option of educating their children with special needs in public schools rather than in special schools; and *(c)* educators are no longer allowing students with special needs, such as those with learning disabilities or emotional problems, to drop out of school but are instead encouraging them to stay.

- Though the goals of inclusion are inarguably noble, in reality the system may present some difficulties. Administrators, school boards, teachers, parents and students must work together to ensure the program's success.

Suggestions for Working with a Student with Special Needs

- Acquire all the information you can about the student, including strengths and weaknesses, from the parents, special education teacher, administration, board of education and the student.

- Establish the reason for placing the student with special needs in your classroom. Make sure the reason is appropriate for the student.

- Though it is not necessary to attend an entire staffing for a student, you should be present when the student's IEP is being developed. The participants, particularly the parents, may have an unrealistic view of their child's abilities. You can provide a better perspective of what can and cannot be achieved based on the student's strengths and weaknesses, your capabilities and the support available. If you cannot attend the meeting, ask to be briefed on the goals that were set and the reasons they were chosen.

- If the IEP goals seem unrealistic, request another meeting to set new goals. Do not let others make unreasonable demands of you and do not make unreasonable demands of yourself.

- Get a clear idea of the services expected of you. If you feel a responsibility is beyond your ability or inappropriate for you to perform, voice your reluctance before the student starts your class.

- Check with the union before refusing to perform any special services which seem inappropriate for a classroom teacher. If you are comfortable performing those services, do so.

- Discuss with the school administration and the union any legalities for working with the student with special needs.

- Based on the type of disability, the age of the children involved and the desires of the student and parents, decide whether to prepare your class for the child's arrival. Some disabilities are immediately evident, others become evident as the school year progresses, and others are unnoticeable. Some disabilities, such as epilepsy, may be frightening and require the students' assis-

5

tance in getting help. The parents of the child with the disability may want to come to school to talk to the class; the child may want to come along; the parents may prefer to have the teacher talk to the students; or the parents may prefer to keep the disability confidential. In any case, respect the parents' wishes. If the disability is to be discussed, ensure that the students receive a truthful representation of the new student and are allowed to ask questions and voice concerns. Encourage the class to accept differences and consider their classmate worthy of support and friendship, rather than attempting to minimize the student's problems.

- In most cases the student with special needs can and should be held to the same standards for classwork and behavior as the rest of the class. It is, rather, the support to achieve those standards that will require special service. In cases in which the disability excludes reaching normal expectations, the teacher must modify assignments, grades, behavioral demands and the classroom, as necessary.

- Decide if you are making accommodations or modifications. Accommodations are changes that do not alter the content or expectations but may change the way the work is produced. Modifications are alterations of content and/or expectations.

- Document the student's progress and failures.

- Accomplish the goals and objectives of the student's IEP to the best of your ability. Do as much as you can and do the best that you can. The fact that a goal is stated on the IEP does not mean that it must be accomplished; it means that it must be attempted.

- Ask the special education teacher, the special education aid and the parents of the student for suggestions about working with the student.

- If you feel a classroom aid is necessary, request one. Enlist the help of colleagues, parents, administration and other students when necessary.

- If an aid is assigned to the student with special needs, work out the details of daily class operation before the aid begins.

- An aid need not be limited to working with the student with special needs. Work out a situation that best serves primarily the student with special needs but also the entire class.

- If the relationship with the aid becomes difficult, maintain professional standards and avoid any action that would harm the aid's effectiveness. Expect the same from the aid.

- Always remember that you still have a class of regular students who also need your attention.

- If the placement of the student with special needs is not working out, discuss the situation with the special education teacher and the school administrator. Get suggestions for better methods of working with the student. If the situation persists, request the administrator call another staffing to discuss a change of services or placement.

Suggestions for Helping the Student with Special Needs Fit into Class

- Greet all students at the door as they enter.

- Call on all students by name.

- Try to call on every student at least once a day.

- Criticize all students constructively.

- Do not be reluctant to punish inappropriate behavior if it was in the control of the student with special needs.

- Have conversations with the student with special needs.

- Give the student with special needs classroom responsibilities.

Glossary

adventitious – accidental, not inherent, occurring in an unusual way

Americans with Disabilities Act (1990) – Public Law 101–336 which extends civil rights to individuals with disabilities

at-risk – a type of student with a higher than average chance of developing a disability

disability – a limitation

due process – the right of families and school boards to get mediation in order to resolve disagreements about services to be provided for a student with special needs

exceptionality – a quality or situation which prohibits a student from receiving his educational needs in a regular classroom

handicap – a limitation imposed by the environment on a person who has a disability or by people's attitude toward the disability

Individualized Education Program / Plan (IEP) – a program drawn up at a staffing to map out the delivery of special services to a student with special needs

Individualized Family Service Plan (IFSP) – the plan developed to help nurture the abilities of children with disabilities from birth to age two

Individuals with Disabilities Education Act (IDEA) (1975) – Public Law 94-142 with supporting legislation, most currently Public Law 105-17 (1997), mandating the right to an appropriate education for all students regardless of their special needs

integrated classroom – a classroom that has both non-disabled and disabled students

interdisciplinary team – a group of educators from different areas, such as a regular classroom teacher, a special education teacher, a school nurse, a social worker, a psychologist, etc., who are responsible for developing an educational plan for a student with special needs

itinerant teacher – a teacher who does work at several schools, usually with students with special needs

least restrictive environment (LRE) – a situation as close in nature as possible to the regular classroom for a student with special needs

mainstreaming – a program in which students with special needs take classes in a regular classroom without receiving special services

multi-disciplinary conference / staffing (MDC / MDS) – a formal meeting of parents and educators at which a specific student's educational needs are discussed and a program developed to aid in the student's education

nondiscriminatory evaluation – the principle that schools must conduct evaluations in a manner which is objective and culturally sensitive

normalization – emphasis on conventional attitudes and behavior in the school setting for students with disabilities

8

paraprofessional – a person who works with the teachers and the students to provide support services

pull-out program – a program in which a student is taken from the regular classroom to receive special help

Regular Education Initiative (REI) – the proposal that special education services be provided in the regular classroom with disabled and non-disabled students attending together

residential facility – a specialized school where the students live and attend class

resilient child – a student who, in spite of a multitude of health and/or environmental problems, manages to cope beyond expectations

resource room – a special room in a school where students with special needs go on a regular basis to get extra help with schoolwork

screening – a basic evaluation of a large group of students devised to locate those who may have a disability and will require further testing

Section 504 of the Rehabilitation Act (1975) – a section of the act that provides that no otherwise qualified individual with a disability may be discriminated against in such places as school and work

special education – additional and specialized services given to a student who would not be able to reach his or her potential in school without them

teacher aid – an adult assigned to provide support to a regular classroom teacher, a special education teacher, an individual student with special needs or a small group of students with special needs

Technology-Related Assistance to Individuals with Disabilities Act (1991) – a federal law which authorizes money to the states to set up a network for providing assistive technology to people with disabilities

transitional services – services to help students with special needs adjust to work and to living after finishing high school

zero reject – the principle which prohibits any student with a disability from being denied a free and appropriate education

Reference Books

Gearhart, Bill R., Mel W. Weishahn, and Carol J. Gearhart. *The Exceptional Student in the Classroom.* 6th ed. Englewood Cliffs, NJ: Prentice-Hall, 1996.

Heward, William L. *Exceptional Children: An Introduction to Special Education.* 5th ed. Englewood Cliffs, NJ: Prentice-Hall, 1996.

Meyen, Edward L. *Exceptional Children in Today's Schools.* 3rd ed. Denver, CO: Love Publishing Company, 1996.

Turnbull, Ann, H. Rutherford Turnbull, and Michael Wehmeyer. *Exceptional Lives: Special Education in Today's Schools.* 5th ed. Saddle River, NJ: Prentice-Hall, 2005.

Wright, Peter W.D., and Pamela Darr Wright. *Wrightslaw: Special Education Law.* Hartfield, VA: Harbor House Law Press, 2004.

Web Sites

Best of Inclusion
www.inclusion.com

The Inclusion Network
www.inclusion.org

Internet Special Education Resources
www.iser.com

Kids Health
www.kidshealth.org

National Association for Dissemination of Disability Research
www.ncddr.org

National Early Childhood Technical Assistance System (NEC-TAS)
www.nectas.unc.edu

The National Information Center for Children and Youth with Disabilities
www.nichy.org

National Institute of Health
www.nih.gov

Publishers of Special Education Material
www.cec.sped.org/fact/publisher

Reed Martin
www.reedmartin.com

Rights and Responsibilities of Parents and Children with Disabilities
www.childdevelopmentinfo.com

Wrights Law
www.wrightslaw.com

Chapter II

Students
with
Learning
Disabilities

Definition

The term "specific learning disability" means a disorder in one or more of the basic psychological processes involved in understanding or in using language, spoken or written, which disorder may manifest itself in imperfect ability to listen, think, speak, read, write, spell, or do mathematical calculations. Such term includes such conditions as perceptual disabilities, brain injury, minimal brain dysfunction, dyslexia, and developmental aphasia. Such term does not include a learning problem that is primarily the result of visual, hearing, or motor disabilities, of mental retardation, of emotional disturbance, or of environmental, cultural, or economic disadvantage.

—IDEA

Important Facts about Students with Learning Disabilities

- The term "learning disabilities" applies to a wide range of problems in the areas of oral expression, listening comprehension, written expression, basic reading ability, reading comprehension, mathematical calculation and mathematical reasoning, and the cognitive processes of perception, attention, memory, metacognition and organization. Learning disabilities may affect one of these areas or many in varying ranges of severity.

- Learning disabilities can be detected by testing students who are having academic problems. Two tests often given are the Illinois Test of Psycholinguistic Abilities (ITPA) and the Marianne Frostig Developmental Test of Visual Perception (Frostig).

- About 51 percent, by far the largest percentage, of students receiving special education services are categorized as learning disabled.

- The ratio of boys to girls with learning disabilities is about three to one.

- The incidence of certified learning disabilities varies from state to state and district to district because there is no standard criteria for granting special education services.

- Although neurological and genetic effects are widely explored as the source of learning disabilities, the causes are generally unknown and may be numerous.

- Unlike other disabilities, learning disabilities are more likely to be discovered by a teacher than a parent because many learning processes are first applied at school.

- There is no such thing as a profile of a student with learning disabilities. The only commonalities are the students' frustration and lack of academic achievement.

- A child with a learning disability does not achieve at a level appropriate to age or ability.

- Many students with learning disabilities also have problems in developing social and behavioral skills.

- There is a tendency for students with learning disabilities to attribute failure to their stupidity or bad luck.

- Learning disabilities are often difficult to discover in a student because the student has developed the ability to avoid answering questions and to guess correctly from contextual clues.

- There is often a behavioral overlay with students that have learning disabilities. It is largely due to the frustration of not understanding or the inability to work at the same rate as other students.

- Many students with learning disabilities develop depression as a result of their feelings of inadequacy, ineptitude and frustration.

- Some students are both gifted and learning disabled. A teacher should watch for flashes of intelligence that may be masked by learning problems.

- A student with learning disabilities misses social cues the same way learning cues are missed and, therefore, often has problems developing social skills.

- The educational prognosis for students with learning disabilities is not good. Many drop out of school because of frustration with their inability to do the work, lack of desire to produce the additional effort or lack of social success.

- Students with learning disabilities, whether they graduate or not, often remain at entry level positions in the workplace.

- Students should be guided to having as many successful experiences as possible.

Characteristics of Students with Learning Disabilities

- Exhibit a discrepancy between perceived ability and performance (the most revealing characteristic).

- Achieve at an uneven rate, sometimes years apart, from one area of learning to another (the second most revealing characteristic).

- Exhibit a discrepancy between listening comprehension and reading comprehension.

- Display a variety of avoidance behaviors.

- Become increasingly disinterested in school.

In reading

- Have difficulty in oral reading

- Make common reading errors, such as letter reversals (dig for big), word reversals (rat for tar), inversions (mine for wine), transportations (felt for left) and substitutions (house for home).

- Have trouble with small words (in, at, an, if, is, etc.).

- Guess, sometimes wildly, at words (individual for industrious),

- Have poor comprehension in silent reading.

- Read slowly.

In writing

- Mix print and cursive.

- Mix upper and lower case letters.

- Make letters in varying sizes.

- Spell poorly with some words very badly misspelled.

- Use vocabulary below their age level.

- Have poor handwriting.

- Make irregular and crooked margins.

- Display a gap between ability to speak and ability to write.

- Make numerous mistakes when copying.

- Mix up word order.

In speaking and conversing

- Forget names of people and familiar objects.
- Use the wrong word to name or explain something.
- Have difficulty putting thoughts into words.
- Respond inappropriately.
- Have problems discriminating sounds.
- Do not fully understand when to talk and when to listen in conversations.

In math

- Lack the ability to apply calculating processes consistently.
- Copy numbers inaccurately.
- Have problems estimating size, distance or amount of money needed for a purchase.
- Have great difficulty interpreting word problems.
- Have difficulty distinguishing pertinent from unnecessary information.

In thought processes

- Have poor memory.
- Have problems keeping several things in their mind at the same time.
- Have difficulty generalizing.
- Have problems understanding abstract concepts, such as democracy or justice.
- Have difficulty putting information into sequence.
- Have difficulty retrieving answers from memory.
- Have poor concept of time.
- Confuse left and right.
- Judge distance poorly.

In classroom procedures
- Frequently guess at answers.
- Do not complete work.
- Are messy.
- Lose materials needed for classwork.
- Do not show signs of understanding when work is explained.
- Have difficulty following directions.

In organization
- Have problems knowing time and date.
- Have problems managing time.
- Have difficulties finding possessions.
- Have difficulties carrying out a plan.
- Are hesitant to make decisions.
- Are reluctant to set priorities.
- Have problems sequencing.

In self-esteem and behavior
- Feel stupid.
- Have low frustration tolerance.
- Have negative attitudes.
- Engage in acting-out behaviors.
- Have poor social skills resulting in low social acceptance.
- Misinterpret social cues.

In body movement
- Lag behind in fine muscle coordination.
- Lack rhythm of movement.

Suggestions for Working with a Student with Learning Disabilities

Because there is such a wide variety of learning disabilities, it is important to discuss the particular student with learning disabilities with the special education teacher or consultant and work out an individualized plan of action. Use the following suggestions as a general reference.

- Instill confidence by assuring the student that success can be achieved.

- Recognize the student as the class authority in any topic and call on him periodically to demonstrate his knowledge. (Each child should be recognized as the authority on some topic).

- Ask the student what accommodations he needs to help him work in class.

- Encourage the parents to establish an area of their child's life in which the child can feel appreciated and special.

In classwork

- Focus on strengthening skills rather than just helping the student to complete individual assignments.

- Have the student work with computer programs specifically designed for students with learning disabilities. (There are many.)

- Arrange for group and peer tutoring.

- Arrange for parents to tutor their child at home. Emphasize work that will reinforce the day's lesson.

In reading

- Identify reading problems as early as possible. Children can be helped to overcome reading disabilities. The earlier the process is started, the better.

- Teach the student to accept that she will have to work harder in school, but can reach the same level of achievement as the students without learning disabilities.

- Help the student practice phonemes, build vocabulary and increase comprehension.

- Have the student read aloud with a skilled reader who can make corrections immediately. This will give the student instant feedback so he can learn from his mistakes.

- Allow the students to chose the books they want to read.

- Provide high interest materials.

- Make sure the student knows the sound of each letter and letter blends. Practice word attacks.

- Teach vocabulary in context.

- Use flash cards to build vocabulary and improve word recognition.

- Suggest that the student place a ruler or straightedge under the line being read to help keep the place.

- For better readability, print assignments on light-colored paper rather than bright white paper. A colored plastic overlay on white paper will serve the same purpose.

- Have the student read a paragraph and then paraphrase it.

- Guide the student through the who, what, when, why and where of the reading.

- Develop questions for the reading selections in which the reader must understand the feelings of the characters. Ask the student to project likely reactions.

- Have the student read silently while listening to the book on tape.

- Ask the student if he would like to read aloud but do not insist on it. If possible, give the student the reading assignment the day before to practice.

- See if large print books are helpful.

- Periodically have choral reading with the entire class.

- Have the student read easy books to younger children.

In writing

- If the student is having trouble writing, suggest using a thicker pencil or pen.

- Allow the student to keep a chart of letters and numbers to check writing accuracy.

- Provide writing exercises with adequate repetition.
- Allow the student to choose whether to print or use cursive.
- Dictate short sentences for the student to write that are already printed on the student's paper but are covered over. Have the student compare what he wrote with what you wrote on the paper.
- Allow collaborative writing.
- Help the student develop outlines for assigned reports.
- Allow the student to work with a classmate when doing a classroom writing assignment.
- Allow the student ample time to finish. Do not insist that work be handed in when the allotted time is up.
- Teach the student to use a computer keyboard and give assignments which can be done on the computer.
- Have the student keep a journal.
- Consider having the student satisfy some written assignments with either a drawing or a tape recording.

In mathematics

- Develop calculator skills.
- Allow the student to use multiplication and division tables.
- Use manipulatives when teaching new concepts.
- Teach the student how to pay attention to math signs.
- Help the student analyze story problems and convert the words into math symbols.
- If possible, reduce the number of drill problems the student must do.
- Focus on step-by-step procedures for math problems. Provide the student with a model that has numbered steps.
- Provide graph paper to keep numbers aligned.
- Allow the student to work with another student or in a group.
- Allow the student to finish the work for homework.

In academics

- When assigning a major assignment, such as the reading of a novel or a term paper, give the assignment to the student early to allow more time to work on it.

- Break large assignments into several smaller assignments.

- Provide the student with an outline of the lesson.

- Teach the student how to find the topic sentence in each paragraph.

- Maintain a dictionary of spelling words that give the student the most problems.

- Write significant material on the board.

- Make use of self-correcting materials, which provide immediate feedback.

- Teach the student how to take notes.

- Allow the student to tape-record lessons and lectures.

- Allow the student to work with other students who can help with some of the basic study and work procedures.

In test-taking

- Review errors from previous assignments and tests and decide how they can be avoided.

- Give the student additional time.

- Give the student fewer problems or questions.

- Give tests orally.

- When writing instructions for a test, the important points should be printed in bold letters and/or underlined.

- Allow the student to take the test in a different setting.

- Give the student a test that is totally different from the test the rest of the class is taking but more appropriate for him.

- Read the questions to the student and ask the student to paraphrase each one as it is read.

- Allow the student to answer questions aloud into a tape recorder.

- When giving a spelling test, first say the word, then use it in a sentence, then repeat the word.

- Develop alternate methods of assessment.

In perception

- Provide plastic or cloth letters and numbers for a younger student. Let the student trace the letters and numbers with his finger. Have the student practice making the shapes on paper. Have the student walk in an open space to make the shapes of the different letters and numbers.

- Have the student use manipulatives whenever possible.

- Provide concrete examples of different objects discussed in class.

- If a student has difficulty understanding the passage of time, have him watch a secondhand sweep around a watch for one minute. The student could also keep a chart noting how many minutes lessons and activities take to complete.

- Have a student with left/right confusion wear a bracelet or watch and identify the wrist it is on.

In attention

- Have the student sit in the front of the class. If the student is not paying attention, stand near the student.

- Develop a cue, such as "now listen to this" or "listen up," whenever there is something you want the entire class to pay attention to. Train your class to recognize this cue and respond to it.

- Give only one or two directions at a time.

- Bring the entire class to attention before making a transition from one task to another.

In memory

- Help the student to associate concepts with concrete examples.

- Attach or relate new information with previously known information.

- Encourage the student to keep a journal of things he needs to remember and to say the things aloud as he is writing.

- Provide written step-by-step instructions for assignments with multiple steps.

- Ask students to visualize what you are saying.

- Provide mnemonic devices, such as "HOMES" for remembering the Great Lakes (Huron, Ontario, Michigan, Erie, Superior), or develop new ones with the student.

In metacognition

- Develop a program of self monitoring, i.e. every five minutes the student charts what he is doing at that moment (listening, talking, working, playing, day-dreaming, etc.).

- Help the student pay attention and follow directions by being supportive while you are giving the directions. Avoid being demeaning.

- Have the student develop methods for working on problems or tasks and see that the chosen methods are followed.

- Encourage the student to verbalize methods of doing assignments.

In organization

- Teach time management.

- Color-code each subject (red for reading, blue for math, yellow for spelling, etc.) and use that color for folders, textbook covers and workbook covers.

- Check to see that the student is putting away papers in the proper folders or in the correct place in his notebook.

- Have the entire class check on personal supplies every Friday afternoon. Develop a checklist that they can use to see what supplies are needed.

- Check to see that assignments are written in an assignment notebook. Arrange with the parents that you will sign the notebook daily after checking to make sure that all assignments have been recorded and that they will sign the notebook daily after reviewing the work assigned.

- Give students an opportunity to check to see that they are taking home all the necessary books and supplies they will need for the evening. Ask parents to check that their child is coming to school with all the necessary books and supplies.

- End each day with a minute or two for cleaning and organizing desks.

In behavior and sociability

- Assure the student that he is not stupid but has a different way of learning.
- Acknowledge the difficulty of learning academic tasks.
- Make the student feel that help is available.
- Acknowledge work that has been completed.
- Praise success and accomplishment.
- Keep a folder for successful work.
- Teach the student to accept responsibility for his work and behavior.
- Teach the student how impulsive behavior affects other students.
- Train the student to think about an answer instead of giving an answer impulsively.
- If it is necessary to punish, make the punishment immediate, logical and rehabilitative.
- Do not allow other students to tease someone for their disability.
- Have the student work in a group with two or three other students.
- Discuss options in social situations.
- Analyze missed social cues.
- Discuss yielding to peer pressure.
- Provide for and encourage healthy peer interactions.

Glossary

anchored instruction – a method of teaching that engages students by instructing around a topic that is interesting to them

developmental articulation disorder – a deficiency in controlling the rate of speed when speaking *developmental expressive language disorder* – a deficiency in expressing oneself verbally

developmental receptive language disorder – a deficiency in understanding and processing speech

direct instruction – a method of teaching that emphasizes one-on-one instruction that includes demonstrations of new information presented in small quantities, opportunities for practice of new skills and immediate feedback

dyscalculia – a learning disability in mathematics characterized by a consistent lack of ability to remember math rules, transform numbers, perform calculations and/or understand abstract concepts

dysgraphia – a learning disability characterized by difficulty writing by hand

dyslexia – a learning disability characterized by difficulty recognizing and/or comprehending written words

dysphasia – a learning disability characterized by difficulty understanding and processing language

dyspraxia – a learning disability characterized by difficulty in motor planning, resulting in awkward movement

encoding process – the ability to organize information so it can be learned

generalization – the ability to apply what is learned to other settings

metacognition – the ability to self-monitor and evaluate mental performance

perception – the ability to organize and interpret what is experienced through the senses

psychological processes – the functions of the brain, such as memory, auditory perception, visual perception, oral language, written language and thinking, which perceive, interpret and act upon information

Reference Books

Deshler, D., and K. Lenz. *Teaching Adolescents with Learning Disabilities: Strategies and Methods.* Denver, CO: Love Publishing Company, 1966.

Harwell, Joan M. *Complete Learning Disabilities Handbook.* 2nd ed. Hoboken, NJ: Jossey-Bass, 2002.

Smith, S. *No Easy Answers.* New York, NY: Bantam Books, 1995.

Winebrenner, Susan and Pamela Espeland. *Teaching Kids with Learning Difficulties in the Regular Classroom.* Minneapolis, MN: Free Spirit Publishing, 1996.

Web Sites

Hello Friend/Ennis William Cosby Foundation
www.hellofriend.org

International Dyslexic Society
www.interdys.org

Internet Special Education Resources
www.iser.com

L.D. Online
www.ldonline.org

Learning Disabilities Association (LDA)
www.ldanatl.org

National Center for Learning Disabilities
www.ncld.org

Chapter III

Students with Behavior Disorders and Emotional Disturbance

(BD/ED)

- *Students with Aggressive Behaviors*
- *Students with Withdrawn Behaviors*

Definitions

Emotionally disturbed is a condition exhibiting one or more of the following characteristics over a long period of time and to a marked degree that adversely affects a student's educational performance: an inability to learn that cannot be explained by intellectual, sensory, or other health factors; an inability to build or maintain satisfactory interpersonal relationships with peers and teachers; inappropriate types of behavior or feelings under normal circumstances; a general pervasive mood of unhappiness or depression; a tendency to develop physical symptoms or fears associated with personal or school problems.

—IDEA

The term "emotional or behavioral disorder" means a disability that is (i) characterized by behavioral or emotional responses in school programs so different from appropriate age, cultural, or ethnic norms that the responses adversely affect educational performance, including academic, social, vocational or personal skills. Such a disability (a) is more than a temporary, expected response to stressful events in the environment, (b) is consistently exhibited in two different settings, at least one of which is school related, and (c) is unresponsive to direct intervention in general education or the child's condition is such that general education interventions would be insufficient. (ii) Emotional and behavioral disorders can co-exist with other disabilities. (iii) This category mat include children or youth with schizophrenic disorders, affective disorders, anxiety disorders, or other sustained disorders of conduct or adjustment when they adversely affect educational performance in accordance with section (i).

—Steven R. Forness and Jane Knitzer

(Reprinted with permission from *School Psychology Review*, Vol. 21, No. 1, p.13. Copyright 1992 National Association of School Psychiatrists.)

(Although schizophrenia is considered a type of emotional disturbance, it is more appropriately for educational purposes included in Chapter XII – Students with Severe and Multiple Disabilities.)

Important Facts about Students with BD/ED

- School districts use different terms to categorize students with behavior disorders and emotional disturbance. Matching each word from the left column with each word from the right column enumerates most of the terms used.

behaviorally	disturbed
emotionally	impaired
socially	handicapped
personally	maladjusted
	disordered
	conflicted

- Though special education programs may group students with emotional disturbance and students with behavior disorders together, the two are quite different. Behavior disorders refer to conditions characterized by aggressive anti-social behavior. Emotional disturbance refers to problems developed due to poor parenting, poor coping skills and stress. Although students with behavior disorders are often harder to control in the classroom, students with emotional disturbance are generally harder to treat.

- Students with BD/ED have the highest drop out rate (about 50 percent).

- The characteristic behavior of children with behavior disorders or emotional disturbance is vague and imprecise. It is therefore necessary for teachers to use their professional judgment when deciding if a student should be screened for these conditions. The intensity, duration, frequency and age appropriateness of a student's behavior should be considered.

- The teacher would be notified if a student is diagnosed with BD/ED. These medical and psychiatric diagnoses are made by doctors and clinicians and should never be made by a classroom teacher.

- The most psychologically devastating factor in a child's experience is rejection. Children who have a history of being rejected will make their situation worse by engendering more rejections. A teacher can help such a child greatly by being accepting.

- The school counselor, special education teacher, parents, school nurse or family doctor may provide specific instructions for working with a student with BD/ED. Instructions from these sources should take precedence over the more generalized suggestions listed in this text.

• If a student exhibits the characteristics of a behavior disorder or an emotional disturbance, but the behavior does not interfere with schoolwork, the student may require outside help but does not need special education services.

• Although some emotional disorders are physiological, it is still possible to modify and control behavior.

• Both the regular teacher and the special education teacher have the primary task of presenting the educational material. Modifying behavior should be secondary.

• Treatment of emotional disorders is based on two schools of thought:

1. the psychoanalytical model (developed by Sigmund Freud) assumes the disorders are a result of conflicts in the unconscious and that treatment depends on uncovering and resolving these conflicts; and

2. the behavioral model (developed by B.F. Skinner) assumes the disorders result from faulty learning and that treatment depends on controlling the environment to teach more appropriate responses.

• Working with students with behavioral disorders and emotional disturbance is significantly different than working with children with other types of disabilities because:

1. there is no need to modify the school work;

2. students play an active role in the severity of the disability;

3. the teacher can play a role in the improvement of the disability;

4. as difficult and disruptive as the students are capable of being, if they become connected to the teacher they are equally capable of being loyal and protective;

5. teachers can exert control on the frequency and extent of the student's problems;

6. parents are not necessarily allies in helping their children to improve;

7. the teacher must separate the student as a person from the behavior;

8. the variety of behaviors and symptoms is vast;
9. the degree of the disorder is difficult to quantify; and
10. the student is capable of drawing the teacher into the disability.

- Students with BD/ED are sometimes holding in large amounts of anger and frustration. When this erupts it can result in destruction of property and harm to self and others. Often the students are frightened of becoming out of control and begin to leave clues in hopes that an adult will discover them and help them get under control again.

- If the student fails to attain a set goal, the teacher should not take it personally. The student is most likely trying to hurt himself or someone he knows or, if trying to hurt or frustrate the teacher, he is doing it for a reason that may have nothing to do with the teacher.

Characteristics of Students with BD/ED

- View the world and surrounding events only in relation to themselves.
- Go to great lengths to avoid what is unpleasant.
- Engage in self-defeating behaviors.
- Manipulate others to achieve own ends.
- Make poor personal choices.
- Lack insights into personal problems.
- Often choose short-term solutions over long-term solutions.
- Require immediate gratification.
- Need excitement and stimulation.
- Associate with deviant peers.

Characteristics of Students with Undiagnosed BD/ED

- Lack interest in school and schoolwork.
- Do not complete schoolwork.
- Have poor relationships with peers.

- Argue with adults.
- Behave inappropriately for age group.
- Exhibit absent, inappropriate or frequently intense feelings.
- Lack interest or concern for others.
- Repeat unnecessary movements.
- Are frequently truant.
- Are frequently anxious.
- Insist on perfection.
- Obsess over seemingly minor problems.
- Show poor grooming and health habits.
- Avoid others.
- Frequently misbehave.
- Are frequently in the center of trouble, though appearing not to be a part of it.
- Frequently complain and make negative comments.
- Are frequently the subject of complaints and negative comments from classmates.
- Overemphasize or lack emphasis of self.
- Frequently complain of physical ailments.

Students with Aggressive Behaviors

Characteristics of Students with Aggressive Behaviors

- Argue often.
- Lack control.
- Become easily frustrated.
- Have tantrums.
- Set fires.
- Tease and provoke others.
- Steal.

- Swear.
- Interrupt.
- Fight.
- Are often disruptive.
- Engage in power struggles.

Characteristics of Students with Violent Behaviors

- Frequently lose temper.
- Frequently fight and lack remorse.
- Vandalize and damage personal property.
- Abuse drugs and/or alcohol.
- State plans to commit violence.
- Enjoy hurting animals.
- Carry and display weapons.

Suggestions for Working with a Student with Aggressive Behaviors

- Be firm in providing structure.
- Be clear about expectations.
- Be patient and calm during outbursts.
- Do not be afraid to confront a student about inappropriate behavior. It is easier to confront than to let it go and see the behavior again.
- Be fair and logical in giving consequences.
- Have the student work with other students who are not easily intimidated.
- Model good behavior.
- Inform the student when behavior is inappropriate and review what the appropriate behavior is.
- For students who have anger outbursts, work out a plan with

them for handling the outbursts. Include a consequence for failure to follow the plan.

- Do not get angry unless you are the target or the victim of an inappropriate act. If this is the case, get angry and explain to the student the results of his action. Condemn the action but not the student. Seek restitution rather than retribution.

- Try not to get involved in power struggles unless there is a safety factor involved. It is better to model good behavior than to try to force the student to perform it.

- Work on improving social skills.

- Compliment appropriate behavior.

- Assign responsibilities and compliment jobs well done.

- Assure the student of individual worth and value to the class.

- Maintain high expectations.

- Avoid being drawn into the student's personal life. Arrange for the student to meet with the school counselor if the student attempts to discuss personal problems.

- Do not take personally any statements that the student has made in anger.

- Avoid acting on behalf of the student or doing special favors.

- Do not feel fear, anger, pity or vengefulness towards the student.

- Do not warn and threaten. Have rules and punishments in place. Exercise them consistently.

- Do not get involved in debates over whether a rule has been broken or about who is the guilty party. Decide and exercise your authority.

Suggestions for Use of a Time-Out Room

- Time-out rooms should be used for students who need respite time. They should not be used for punishments.

- Students in a time-out room must always be under the observation and supervision of an adult.

- Students should not be assigned a specific length of time to stay in the time-out room. They should remain as long as they need to get themselves under control.

• Students who are sent to time-out frequently are not benefitting from the time-out, and another consequence must be found.

Students with Withdrawn Behaviors

Characteristics of Students with Withdrawn Behaviors

• Are quiet in class and shy toward others.

• Prefer to be left alone.

• Seem fearful.

• Appear unhappy.

• Lack energy.

• Are overly anxious.

• Are often unable to focus.

• Exhibit obsessive and compulsive behaviors.

• Are frequently absent.

• Make self-depreciating remarks.

• Inflict injury on themselves.

• May be suicidal.

Suggestions for Working with a Student with Withdrawn Behaviors

• Insist on good work.

• Be clear in your expectations.

• Help the student develop social skills.

• Encourage personal correspondence between the student and teacher, perhaps in the form of a journal.

• Be warm and accepting. Make the student feel a sense of worth.

• Call the student by name before giving a direction.

• Have the student work with another student or a small group of non-threatening students.

- Have an assignment on the board that all students are to begin as soon as they enter the room.

- Protect the student from being teased or belittled.

- If the student becomes overly depressed, allow the student to retreat to a private part of the room or to put her head down on her desk until she feels she is able to rejoin the class. Do not insist that the work be completed at these times but hold the student accountable for completing the work later. Notify the parents and the school counselor if depression is frequent and initiate a plan to manage it.

Suggestions for Working with Students who Threaten Violence, Murder or Suicide

- Recognize a student's hints regarding possible violent behavior. Children who develop violent thoughts and impulses often become scared and afraid of what they might do. When they feel they cannot stop themselves, they begin to drop both verbal and written hints in the hope that some other person, usually an adult, will help them regain control. This is why it is so important that the teacher recognize these hints and help the student control his behavior.

- Encourage your school to have a plan for handling both oral and written statements of violence, murder and suicide. The plan should include the role of the teacher, the person whom the teacher should notify, and the conditions under which school security and/or police should be notified. The plan should consider first the safety of all students and school personnel.

- In most cases, students who make threats are not intending to carry them out. However, the teacher must take all threats seriously and act accordingly.

- If a student makes any statement threatening destruction of property or harm to another student:

  1. question the student as to his intentions,
  2. attempt to get the student to seek other solutions, and
  3. try to keep the student with you until you feel he has regained

control of himself and states he no longer wishes to do this. Do not do this if you feel there is a danger to yourself. Report the incident immediately to school authorities.

- If the student threatens self-harm or suicide immediately:

  1. talk to the student about the enormity of his choice,
  2. insist on the value of living,
  3. relate the student's importance to you and the class,
  4. insist the student tell you he will not do anything rash,
  5. accompany the student to the school counselor, social worker or administrator,
  6. help the student begin relating what he had related to you,
  7. do this even if the student insists it was just a joke, and
  8. make sure the student's parents are notified.

Definitions of Specific Types of BD/ED and Suggestions for Working with a Student Who Has Them

adjustment disorder – a maladaptive reaction to a stressful situation which disappears when the stress is removed

- Offer the student support during times of stress.
- Talk the student through what he is doing while getting him to focus on the nature and cause of the stress.
- Give positive feedback when the situation is resolved.

aggression – the act of disregarding the safety and rights of others in order to promote one's own desires

- Insist the behavior will not be permitted in school.
- Insist the student return or replace inappropriate gains made.
- Enforce the required consequences.
- Help the student find other, more socially acceptable, ways to gain desired ends.

alcohol and drug abuse – the misuse or overuse of alcohol and/or legal or illegal drugs resulting in an encroachment on other aspects of life

• Do not sanction or make any positive references to alcohol or drug use.

• If the student shows any desire to stop, try to get the student into a rehabilitation program with the help of the school counselor and the parents.

anorexia – severe self-starvation

• Be aware of a student's sudden weight loss or preoccupation with weight loss.

• Because this is a very difficult disorder to address, get instructions from the parents or family doctor.

• Allow the student to eat in class even if you have a rule against eating in class.

anxiety disorders – a set of disorders including phobias, panic attacks, post-traumatic stress disorders and obsessive/compulsive disorder in which the student feels an unnecessary amount of fear, worry or uneasiness about everyday activities.

• Be flexible. Do not insist the student always act in the same manner as the rest of the class.

bipolar disorder – severe mood swings that go from mania (extreme excitement) to depression (previously called manic-depression; often mistaken for attention-deficit/hyperactivity disorder)

• Get instructions from the parent or family doctor on what to do if the student goes into a severe mania or depression.

• Expect to be asked to help control the mania but not the depression.

• Expect the student to stay at home when the symptoms, especially the depression, become severe.

bulimia – reoccurring binge eating followed by purging (often related to anorexia)

• Be aware of a student's excessive weight loss or preoccupation with weight loss. Bad breath from purging is a common symptom.• Do not allow the student to go to the washroom unaccompanied, especially after eating.

• Get instructions, if available, from parents or family doctor.

character disorder – acting-out, aggressive disorder in which the student shows little or no regard for others and no feelings of guilt for having done something wrong.

• Refer to the suggestions on aggressive behaviors.

conduct disorder – repetitive persistent patterns of behavior which violate or endanger others, such as inflicting harm on animals or other people, destroying property, lying, stealing and habitually breaking school rules.

• Refer to the suggestions on aggressive behaviors.

depression – depressed mood with loss of interest and lack of pleasure in everyday activities.

• Try to involve the student in activities with others.

• Encourage the student to take pleasure in accomplishments. If depression becomes too strong, allow the student to withdraw for periods of time with supervision from the school counselor, nurse, or special education teacher.

encopresis/enuresis – incontinence of bowels and urine

• Insist on receiving a specific plan from the student's parents or family doctor before accepting the student into your classroom.

• Have student keep a change of clothing available.

impulsivity – the inability to delay gratification and the tendency to act without thinking or considering the results of the action.

- Help the student to consider consequences of actions.

- Insist the student return or replace inappropriate gains made through impulsive behavior or actions.

- Enforce required consequences.

- Place the student in situations where thinking before acting is required.

mania – excessive love or enthusiasm centered on a particular activity or subject

- If the mania is inappropriate for school, intercede by forbidding the student to act out the mania.

- Enforce the required consequences.

- Request directions from the family doctor or special education teacher.

mood disorders – disorders of emotion, elation or depression that dominate one's outlook on life

- Try to teach and model appropriate moods for the activity in progress.

- Encourage the student to express appropriate feelings.

obsessive/compulsive disorder – a pattern of repetitive, persistent and intrusive thoughts (obsessions) and actions (compulsions) which interfere with the daily activity of one's life

- Try to accommodate these actions if not too intrusive or disruptive to the classroom procedures.

- Work with the student to limit the amount of disruption caused.

oppositional defiant disorders – a pattern of negative hostile behavior in which a student defies authority and school rules and may deliberately act in a way to annoy others

- Try to reach the student with positive reinforcements for appropriate behavior. If the student feels at all invested in the teacher, it is possible for the teacher to request, teach and reward more appropriate behaviors.

panic attacks – an overwhelming irrational fear causing heavy, shallow breathing, sweating, rapid heartbeat, and retreat from the feared stimulus

• Stay close to the person having the panic attack and give assurance that the feared object will not cause harm. Wait for attack to pass.

personality disorders – maladaptive behaviors related to perceiving and thinking about oneself in relation to the environment, which result in poor functioning and personal failure and distress

• Expect difficulties when working with the student.

• Consult often with the special education teacher and the school social worker for suggestions to help the student.

• Remember that the student may be choosing to act in self-defeating ways.

• Use punishment judiciously.

phobias – irrational and unwarranted fears

• Try to help the student deal with or overcome the phobia by helping the student approach the fear, understand it and act appropriately. Do not force the student to do this.

pica – the eating of non-food objects such as hair, fingernails, paint chips or cloth.

• Offer the student something more desirable to eat if the student will forego the pica.

post-traumatic stress syndrome – a reaction to an extremely threatening incident after which the student experiences sleep disorders, eating disorders, anxiety and avoidance behavior to a degree that interferes with daily life

• Request specific instructions from the special education teacher or family doctor on how to help the student.

• Avoid putting the student under additional stress.

• Try to involve the student in as much daily classroom activity as possible.

psychopathic personality (anti-social personality disorder) – a disorder characterized by amoral and anti-social behaviors, such as hitting, stealing and/or lying with impulsive, irresponsible and self-serving ends, lack of remorse and little or no regard for others

• Set very clearly defined consequences, inflexible in their execution, for behavior that is inappropriate.

• Watch the student closely.

• Remove the student from class if the behavior becomes too much of a problem.

psychosexual disorders – any disorder involving sexual functioning or sex-typed behavior

• If appropriate, monitor the student's behavior with a clearly defined set of expectations and consequences.

• If an infraction occurs, remove the student from the regular classroom.

• Make sure the standards for the student's behavior are defined with the well-being of the student in mind and not personal philosophies.

school phobia – fear of going to school usually accompanied by anxiety, physical complaints and tiredness

• Try to make the student comfortable in school and en route to and from school.

• If necessary, let the student express fears and concerns about attending.

• If possible, recommend that a program be established to bring the student to school on days when it is difficult to attend voluntarily.

self-mutilation – the practice of habitually inflicting wounds on oneself, considered an expression anger often due to sexual abuse

• Help the student to express feelings in words or writing.

• Refer the student to a therapist if not already in therapy.

separation anxiety disorder – fear of being separated from a parent (usually the mother), common the first few days of school (sometimes difficult to resolve if the anxiety is strong and felt by both the student and the parent)

• Engage the student in activities, and the problem usually goes away by itself as the child becomes accustomed to being away from the parent.

• If the child and the parent are sharing the anxiety, insist the parent leave the area and let the student cry or carry out a tantrum until ready to join the class.

• If the problem persists or if it occurs in an older child, discuss it with the counselor or special education teacher.

Tourette's syndrome – a neurological disorder characterized by motor and vocal tics, such as sudden movements or shouted words (sometimes obscene), sometimes accompanied by learning disabilities, attention-deficit/hyperactivity disorders, obsessive/compulsive disorders and sleep disorders

• Remember that these are involuntary and should not be punished.

• Seat the student away from distractions.

• Provide the student with a study carrel if necessary.

• Allow the student to leave the classroom to go to the bathroom or a safe place if the tics become excessive.

• Do not allow the classmates to tease the student.

Promoting Mental Health in Your Classroom

• Provide the students with a sense of worth and belonging.

• Help the students adapt to change.

- Recognize individual accomplishments.
- Affirm that individual behavior makes a difference.
- Help the students be flexible and resilient.

Maintaining Your Own Mental Health in Difficult Classroom Situations

- Maintain your ability to give and receive affection.
- Be firm with your students without being mean.
- Have one or more people with whom you can openly discuss stressful situations.
- Have access to non-school resources for renewal.
- Try to invest a part of your effort in improving the school as a whole.
- Maintain hope, calm and confidence.
- Behave with openness, optimism and empathy.
- Be able to separate school problems from personal problems.
- Periodically reward yourself for a job well done.

Glossary

affective disorder – mood disorder

Applied Behavior Analysis (ABA) – the idea that a certain behavior follows a certain stimulus; by controlling the environment you can control the behavior

behavior intervention plan (BIP) – a plan that includes positive strategies, programs and curriculum modifications that address targeted behaviors

behavior modification – a method of shaping behavior by rewarding wanted responses and ignoring or punishing unwanted responses

contingency contracting – an agreement that performing or giving up specific behaviors will result in an agreed upon reward

DSM-IV (Diagnostic and Statistical Manual of Mental Disorders, 4th ed.) – the manual developed by the American Psychiatric Association for classifying emotional disturbances

eating disorders – an obsessive interest in food intake, weight gain and loss, dieting or body image—most often overeating, anorexia and bulimia

egocentric – a view of all things in relation to oneself

modeling – giving a demonstration of a desired behavior

projective test – a test, such a the Rorschach Test (inkblots) or the Thematic Aperception Test, in which responses are determined by experiences and state of mind

socialized aggression – aggressive and disruptive behavior learned and performed in a group setting, such as a gang activity

tic – a sudden involuntary spasmatic movement or utterance

Reference Books

Gimpel, Gretchen A. and Melissa L. Holland. *Emotional and Behavioral Problems of Young Children: Effective Interventions in the Preschool and Kindergarten Years.* New York, N.Y.: The Guilford Press, 2003.

Lane, Kathleen Lynne, Frank M. Gresham and Tam E. O'Shaughnessy. *Interventions for Children With or At-Risk for Emotional and Behavioral Disorders.* Boston, MA: Allyn & Bacon, 2001.

Newcomer, Phyllis L. *Understanding and Teaching Emotionally Disturbed Children and Adolescents.* 3rd ed. Austin, TX: PRO-ED, Inc., 2002.

Quay, Herbert C. and Anne E. Hogan. *Handbook of Disruptive Behavior Disorders.* London, UK: Kluwer Academic/Plenum Publishers, 1999.

Yanoff, Jerome C. *The Classroom Teacher's Trouble-Shooting Handbook.* Chicago, IL: Arthur Coyle Press, 1999.

Web Sites

Anxiety Disorders Association of America
www.ADAA.org

Mental Health Infosource
www.mhsource.com

National Alliance for the Mentally Ill
www.nami.org

National Association of Anorexia Nervosa and Associated Eating
Disorders
www.anad.org

National Institute of Mental Health (NIMH)
www.nimh.nih.gov

National Mental Health Association
www.nmha.org

Suicide Prevention Action Network
www.span.org

Chapter IV

Students with Attention-Deficit/ Hyperactivity Disorder (AD/HD)

- *Students with Predominantly Inattentive Type AD/HD*

- *Students with Predominantly Hyperactive-Impulsive Type and Combined Type AD/HD*

Definition

The essential feature of Attention-Deficit / Hyperactivity Disorder is a persistent pattern of inattention and / or hyperactivity-impulsivity that is more frequent and severe than is typically observed in individuals at a comparable level of development (Criterion A). Some hyperactive-impulsive or inattentive symptoms that cause impairment must have been present before age 7 years, although many individuals are diagnosed after the symptoms have been present for a number of years (Criterion B). Some impairment from the symptoms must be present in at least two settings (e.g., at home and at school or work) (Criterion C). There must be clear evidence of interference with developmentally appropriate social, academic, or occupational functioning (Criterion D). The disturbance does not occur exclusively during the course of a Pervasive Developmental Disorder, Schizophrenia, or other Psychotic Disorder and is not better accounted for by another mental disorder (e.g., a mood disorder, Anxiety Disorder, Dissociative Disorder, or Personality Disorder (Criterion E).

— American Psychiatric Association

(Reprinted with permission from the *Diagnostic and Statistical Manual of Mental Disorders*, Fourth edition. Copyright 1994 American Psychiatric Association.)

Important Facts about Students with AD/HD

- Attention-deficit/hyperactivity disorder is a medical diagnoses. This diagnosis should never be made by a teacher.

- The words "hyperactive" and "hyper" are overused and misused. A child can be overactive without being hyperactive.

- If an environment could be designed that would be particularly torturous to an AD/HD student, it would be the everyday regular classroom.

- A teacher's attitude, willingness to help and flexibility are key to the success of the student with AD/HD more so than to any other type of student.

- Students with AD/HD have a disability. They are not choosing to act the way they do. Most of them do not like the way they are and would change their behaviors if they could.

- Working with children with AD/HD can be very frustrating for a teacher. Although it may seem that they are testing the teacher's structure to see what they can get away with, they are not. Neither are they being defiant.

- Some students view their label of AD/HD as an excuse to misbehave and/or avoid work. AD/HD should instead be viewed as a disorder which must be overcome to pursue an education.

- A teacher who suspects a student has undiagnosed AD/HD should document the student's behavior and consult with the school counselor or special education teacher.

- AD/HD cannot be cured, but it can be managed.

- It is extremely important that the student with AD/HD is given opportunities to experience success in the classroom.

- Approximately 15 percent of AD/HD children are predominantly inattentive. Approximately 85 percent of students with AD/HD have the combined type.

- Approximately 20 percent of students with AD/HD also have some form of a learning disability. About 33 percent of students with AD/HD also have some form of a behavior disorder. About 35 percent of students seeing a therapist on a regular basis are being treated for AD/HD. This represents the largest percentage of all childhood psychological disorders.

- About 20 percent of students with AD/HD have problems with depression or anxiety. The depression stems from their feelings of ineptitude, frustration and social isolation.

- Students with AD/HD can be highly imaginative and creative.

- Some students with AD/HD will hyperfocus on subjects which interest them and can spend hours focusing on that subject to the exclusion of other demands. Video games are a good example of this.

- Students with AD/HD are prone to having accidents.

- Students with AD/HD try harder in school when they feel the teacher likes them.

- Problems caused by AD/HD cannot be resolved but can be eased.

- A behavioristic program for a student with AD/HD is more effective than psychotherapy.

51

Suggestions for Working with a Student with AD/HD

- Focus not only on helping the student modify his behavior but on working around his behavior while he is learning to modify it.

- Support the student emotionally and do not let him get down on himself.

- Use visual presentations rather than oral ones.

- Give project-oriented assignments.

- Schedule most of the academics in the morning.

- Post the classroom rules and the weekly schedule.

- Ask the student what helps him the most.

- Help the student to set and monitor personal goals.

- Teach time management.

- Build opportunities for the student to be out of his seat during the lessons.

- Make sure the student has all the necessary study materials.

- Give only one or two instructions at a time.

- Have the student repeat instructions aloud.

- Talk through the academic processes, such as mathematical processes. Teach the student to do this alone.

- Color-code the student's textbooks, workbooks and folders by subject.

- Have the class answer questions with choral responses instead of calling on individuals.

- If possible, allow the student to keep a set of textbooks at home.

- Help the student make transitions from one subject to another by limiting transition time.

- For major assignments, such as a report, set deadlines for each phase or component.

- Have the student write all assignments in an assignment note-book. Review and sign the notebook at the end of the day and have the parent sign it at home.

- Highlight directions on work sheets and tests.

- At the end of the day allow a few minutes for all the students to organize their desks and work.

- Set up classroom routines and try to stay with them. Prepare the students for exceptions.

- Use behavioral contracts that specify the amount of time allotted for activities.

- Predetermine consequences for infractions of rules.

- Alternate highly interesting and less interesting tasks.

- Teach keyboard skills.

- Give the student rewards such as computer time and free reading time rather than candy or other sweets.

- Allow the student to move around the classroom if it can be done without disturbing other students.

- Help the student understand appropriate and inappropriate behavior.

- Give feedback frequently.

- Do not become exasperated or display frustration.

- Communicate frequently with the parents.

Students with Predominantly Inattentive Type AD / HD

Characteristics of Students with Predominantly Inattentive Type AD/HD (also called ADD or IN [Inattentive])

- Often appear to be daydreaming or staring.

- Are often confused about what to do or what directions mean.

- Appear apathetic and unmotivated.

- Seem slow-moving.

- May not grasp details or understand the complete picture.

- May concentrate on something extraneous.

- Make many careless mistakes.

- Show reluctance to engage in tasks which require commitment.
- Are unassertive, polite and docile.
- Attempt to bond with other students but are seldom successful.
- May go unreported because they don't pose behavior problems.

Suggestions for Working with a Student with Predominantly Inattentive Type AD/HD

- Seat the student in close proximity with others.
- Assign a study-buddy to work with the student.
- Assign as much group work as possible.
- Stand near the student's desk during some of your presentations.
- Make eye contact while giving verbal instructions.
- Use introductory phrases, such as "listen up" or "pay attention to this."
- Ask the student to repeat instructions back.
- If you must repeat directions, do it calmly, without anger or sarcasm.
- Use worksheets and help the student underline the most significant material.
- Provide the structure and support necessary to complete the work.
- Try to call on the student when she is paying attention.
- Give positive feedback for correct answers.
- Allow extra time to complete work.
- Write assignments on the board as you give them. Leave them on the board for a while. Give the students advance notice of erasure.
- Break large assignments into smaller assignments.
- Have a set time when the students enter their homework assignments into their assignment notebooks. Allow the students to exchange assignment books with a partner to check their partner's accuracy.
- Try to apply the same academic standards as those for the rest

of the class but prepare to be flexible.

- Teach the student to monitor behavior.
- Make the student feel comfortable about asking for help.

Students with Predominantly Hyperactive-Impulsive and Combined Type AD/HD

Characteristics of Students with Predominantly Hyperactive-Impulsive and Combined Type AD/HD (also called HI [hyperactive, impulsive] and CB [combined])

- Often fidget and squirm.
- Often get out of seat.
- Display excessive physical activity.
- Are bossy and irritating and do not play well with others.
- Cannot play or work quietly.
- Talk excessively.
- Burst out with answers before the question is completed.
- Have difficulty awaiting turn.
- Interrupt.
- Act rude.
- Fail to pick up social cues.
- Show off.
- Are rebellious and short-tempered.
- Act immature.
- Have frequent emotional outbursts.
- Have poor organizational skills.
- Often forget or lose assignments.
- See events in black or white.
- Have poor self-image.

Suggestions for Working with a
Student with Predominantly Hyperactive-Impulsive and
Combined Type AD/HD

- Do not assume the goal for a hyperactive student is to keep him in his seat working with a minimum of distraction. Rather, strive to have the student working creatively and productively.

- Assign the student a seat at the periphery of the class near the front but away from the windows.

- If necessary, provide a second seat in a relatively empty part of the room where the student may sit whenever necessary. Supply the desk with a complete set of books and essential supplies. Erect partitions that seclude the desk from the rest of the class. Teach the student to record his own behavior with periodic checks (e.g., once every five minutes).

- If possible, alternate in-seat and moving-around activities, allowing more moving-around activities in the afternoon.

- If a student has a problem with a particular behavior, such as talking without first raising a hand to be recognized, place a reminder (a note or picture) on the corner of the student's desk.

- Expect that some days will be better than others.

- Emphasize use of tactile objects and hands-on learning.

- Assign tasks that require the student to move around the room or building.

- Teach relaxation techniques.

- Assign activities that can be done in pairs. Then pair the student with a strong well-organized partner.

- Look for areas in which the student can appropriately provide leadership.

- Have the student tutor or mentor younger students.

- Stress cooperation over competition.

- Acknowledge good work.

- Use positive reinforcement as much as possible.

- Provide feedback, rewards and punishments immediately. Give

56

tangible rather than verbal rewards whenever possible. A give-and-give-back token system can be effective.

- Use positives and praise more than negatives and punishment.

- If necessary, develop alternative ways to assess progress.

- Give the student a job, such as leaving the room to pick up trash in the hall.

- Provide the student with a list of classroom rules.

- Before recess or a field trip, review the rules that need to be followed.

- Do not punish minor inappropriate behaviors. Rather, chose one or two you really want to work on.

- Do not punish what cannot be controlled.

- Do not remove the student from class. This does not help improve his behavior.

- Help the student through transitions.

- Encourage the student to be involved in sports.

- Never take away PE or recess as a punishment.

- Allow the student to wear headphones that play soothing music or white noise during seat work.

- Have the student wear a watch timer set at five or ten minute intervals to remind him to return to task.

- Give handouts and rely less on having the student copy material from the board.

Medication for Students with AD/HD

- Some medications used in treating AD/HD are Adderal, Concerta, Cylert, Dexadrine, Norpramin, Prozac, Ritalin, Strattera and Tofranil. New medications are presented periodically.

- Children who need medication are started on a weak dosage. If no improvement is shown, the dosage will slightly increase until there is a change in behavior.

- Children taking medication for AD/HD usually receive counseling.

- The most common side effects of medications taken for AD/HD include insomnia, decreased appetite, stomach pains, increased heart rate and irritability.

- Approximately 30 percent of children who try medication for AD/HD respond negatively. Some have no response at all.

- The parents and family doctor will usually ask the teacher to monitor changing behavior in a child who is beginning to take medications.

- If a child responds well to a medication, the teacher and the parents should applaud the child and not the medication. The medication only allows the student to exert his strengths.

- The teacher should be informed of all changes in medication.

- Whether to give medication to children with AD/HD is a controversial topic.

- Some adults feel that medicating children with AD/HD demonstrates the parents' desire to control their child's behavior with an easy fix. They feel the child would be better served if the parents learned to deal with the child's behavior.

- Other adults feel that children with AD/HD would be unreachable both at home and at school were it not for the medication they take.

- Some parents worry that putting their children on medication will increase their likelihood to later engage in substance abuse. However, studies show that children who take medication for AD/HD are less likely to engage in substance abuse.

- Whether to give medication to a child is a family decision that should not involve the teacher. The role of the classroom teacher is to lend support to the parents who must make this difficult decision.

- The classroom teacher should never suggest to parents that their child needs medication.

Glossary

hyperactivity – a condition characterized by excessive energy and movement, much of which is out of control (a medical assessment not a judgment) *impulsivity* – a condition characterized by acting on a thought before thinking out its consequences

psychotropic medication – medication which alters feelings, behavior and perception

Reference Books

Alban-Metcalf, J. *Managing Attention Deficit / Hyperactivity Disorder in the Inclusive Classroom.* London, UK: David Fulton Publishers, 2001.

Dendy, Chris A. Ziegler. *Teenagers with ADD: A Parents' Guide.* Bethesda, MD: Woodbine House, 1995.

Flick, Grad L. *How to Reach and Teach Teenagers with ADHD.* Edison, NJ: Jossey-Bass, 2000.

Greenbaum, Judith and Geraldine Markel. *Helping Adolescents with ADHD & Learning Disabilities: Ready-to-Use Tips, Techniques, and Checklists for School Success.* Edison, NJ: Jossey-Bass, 2000.

Hartman, T. *Attention Deficit Disorder: A Different Perspective.* Lancaster, PA: Underwood Miller, 1993.

Lerner, Janet W., Barbara Lowenthal and Sue R. Lerner. *Attention Deficit Disorders: Assessment and Teaching.* Pacific Grove, CA: Brooks/Cole Publishing Company, 1994.

Mercogliano, Chris. *Teaching the Restless: One School's Remarkable No-Ritalin Approach to Helping Children Learn and Succeed.* Boston, MA: Beacon Press, 2004.

Web Sites

ADDinSchool.com
   www.addinschool.com

AD/HD Support Company
   www.adhdsupportcompany.com

Attention Deficit Disorder Association
   www.add.org

Attention Deficit Information Network
www.addinfonetwork.org

Children and Adults with Attention Deficit Disorders (CHADD)
www.chadd.org

National Resource Center on AD/HD
www.help4adhd.org

One ADD Place
www.oneaddplace.com

Chapter V

Students
with
Autism

- *Higher-Functioning Students with Autism*
- *Lower-Functioning Students with Autism*

Definition

Autism means a developmental disability significantly affecting verbal and nonverbal communication and social interaction, generally evident before the age of 3, that adversely affects educational performance. Other characteristics often associated with autism are engagement in repetitive activities and stereotyped movements, resistance to environmental change or changes in daily routine, and unusual responses to sensory experiences. The term does not apply if a child's educational performance is adversely affected primarily because the child has a serious emotional disturbance.

—IDEA

Important Facts about Students with Autism

- Autism is classified as a pervasive developmental disorder (PDD). This group of disorders also includes Asperger's syndrome, childhood disintegrative disorder, Rett's disorder and pervasive developmental disorders not otherwise specified.

- Contrary to what many believe, students with autism are capable of learning and giving and receiving affection.

- Autism manifests itself in a variety of ways and a range of severity. Some autistic children require constant support because they behave in bizarre ways, such as being out of control or being unable to listen or respond to others. Others require only minimal support because they behave in just a slightly odd way, such as speaking with unusual intonation.

- Approximately 20 percent of autistic children have average or above average intelligence. Approximately 30 percent are considered mildly or moderately retarded. The rest are considered severe or profoundly retarded.

- Higher-functioning people with autism perform normally in making friends, marrying, and maintaining a job.

- Approximately 75 percent of autistic children are boys.

- Many children with autism also have epileptic seizures.

- About half the children with autism do not speak. Many are taught to communicate through sign language or a picture exchange communications system (PECS).

- It is possible for a teacher or teacher aid to form a relationship with a student with autism. To do so they must create a sense of security by being sensitive to the needs of the student and meeting those needs.

- Few people with autism have the ability to remember extraordinary amounts of facts and numbers (islets of competence, previously "idiot savant" or "savant syndrome").

- Because autism severely limits a person's ability to communicate, it is sometimes viewed as a communications disorder.

- Autism most likely has a physiological basis and not a psychological basis, as previously thought.

- Because students with autism can be very difficult to maintain in the regular classroom, the classroom teacher should be expected to do only the best she can under the circumstances.

- No matter how difficult a student with autism may be to maintain, the child still feels joy and pain like any other child.

- The teacher, the aid and the student with autism should take delight in all successes and not feel overly frustrated or guilty about academic goals not reached.

- Although students with autism have the lowest school drop-out rate of any group of exceptional students, only about two-fifths receive a standard high school diploma.

- Many schools have a substantial support network for students with autism which includes the special education teacher, social worker, speech-language therapist, occupational therapist and other adults.

- The idea that autism can be caused by the measles-mumps-rubella (MMR) vaccination has been substantially disproven. Parents should also know that even if there is evidence to the contrary, denying the MMR inoculation puts the child at higher risk of disease.

Characteristics of Students with Autism

In communication
- Engage in little or no speech.

- May repeat phrases heard previously (echolalia).
- May confuse pronouns in the same manner as children just learning to speak.
- May speak with abnormal flow and intonation.
- Will not initiate conversation.
- Will not engage in normal conversation.
- Will not understand sarcasm, irony, double entendres, etc.

In intelligence

- Have little incidental learning.
- Typically have IQs lower than average.
- Have limited ability to generalize information.
- Have few organizational skills.
- Have limited ability for abstract thinking.
- Have limited ability for fantasy.
- May have exceptional ability to memorize trivia.
- May have islets of competence in such areas as drawing, mental math or perfect pitch.

In social relationships

- Prefer to be alone.
- Bond with a limited number of people, usually family members.
- Lack eye contact and have little awareness of the presence of others.
- Do not initiate play.
- Do not form friendships with peers.
- Usually dislike being touched.
- May engage in improper hugging or sexual touching of self and others.
- May, in some cases, present a danger to others (hitting and biting).

In movement

- May be awkward in both posture and fine and gross motor control.

In behavior

- Function best in an environment of routine and predictability.

- Engage in self-stimulating behaviors such as rocking, swinging, hand flapping and self-hitting.

- Swallow non-food objects (pica).

- Become fixated on certain objects.

- Respond unpredictably to everyday events.

- Become easily frustrated and upset, possibly resulting in an outburst.

- Prone to sudden self-destructive violence when upset, such as head-banging, biting or scratching. May also damage the room or harm others, though not intentionally.

- React adversely to certain sounds, such as the hum of a fluorescent light or certain textures, such as some clothing.

- Make no response to a sound or the start of a conversation.

- Have some insensitivity to pain.

- Usually resist normal teaching methods.

Suggestions for Working with a Higher-Functioning Student with Autism

Some students with autism are capable of doing regular or near regular classwork and should be treated accordingly. The following suggestions are for those who cannot:

- Be more concerned with the student's social interactions than with schoolwork.

- Work out a grading system that reflects the progress made by the student. Discuss this with the administration and the student's parents.

- Do not take personally what a student with autism says or does.

- If possible acquire the services of an aid to help the student with autism with organizational tasks and daily functioning.

- Consider scheduling the student for speech and language therapy.
- Recommend occupational and vocational therapy for older students.
- If appropriate, assign the student a study-buddy to help organize, assist with classwork and keep track of work to be done later.
- If the student can cooperate, encourage working in groups.
- Emphasize developing communication skills.
- Help the student learn to verbally express feelings of discomfort.
- Provide the student with a daily schedule. If there are to be any changes to the schedule, inform the student as soon as possible and assure the student that the day will be all right.
- Provide the student with a set of rules which must be followed.
- Watch movies and videos. Discuss what people are saying and feeling.
- Give the student two sets of books, one for home use and one for school.
- Break down assignments into small isolated steps. When one step is mastered, go to the next step.
- Provide guides and examples for any assignments the student finds difficult.
- Gradually increase the number of tasks the student is to perform.
- Emphasize visual presentations of classwork rather than spoken presentations.
- Emphasize computer and keyboard skills.
- Encourage the student to carry a notebook of things to remember to do.
- Highlight important written information.
- Highlight directions on tests.
- Practice real social situations.
- Teach to the student's strengths.

- Do not punish the student for behavior he cannot control.
- Try to involve the student in extra-curricular activities to encourage social interaction.
- Do not rely on the student to deliver messages to his home.

Suggestions for Working with a
Lower-Functioning Student with Autism

- Establish the reasons the student is being placed in your classroom.
- Try to have the student deal with as few adults as possible.
- Request the services of a one-on-one aid who will be responsible for maintaining the daily functioning and appropriate behavior of the student.
- Request the student not be sent to school if the aid is going to be absent. If this is not possible and you are to receive a substitute aid, ask that the aid come early to be briefed on how to help the student.
- Inform the parents if you know you are going to be absent from school.
- Periodically review the student's behavior and progress with the aid. Do not be afraid to constructively critique each other.
- With your administration and the student's parents work out a grading system which will reflect the achievements the student has made.
- Do not make completing classwork or keeping up with learning the primary goal.
- Structure the entire day. Avoid free time.
- Most importantly, teach communication skills, social skills and self-help skills.
- Concentrate on providing a functional curriculum.
- Teach language learning in the student's natural setting emphasizing the most needed vocabulary.
- Give the student a visual schedule—all the activities for the day presented as pictures with descriptive words underneath.

Review the schedule with the student when he arrives.

- If the student has a sensitivity to light, try to lower the lighting. Allow the student to wear a cap with a visor to block overhead lighting. Allow sunglasses.

- Allow the student to use paraphernalia to block excessive stimulation, such as ear plugs, ear phones or nose plugs.

- Encourage interaction between the student and classmates. Post a sign-up sheet for volunteer peer buddies.

- Include the student in as many classroom activities as the student is able to handle.

- Establish a routine.

- If the student becomes fixated on an object, try to work that object into the lesson.

- Put large name tags on the student's desk, chair, locker, coat hook, etc.

- Avoid overwhelming the student. Either show the student what is to be done or tell the student, but do not do both at the same time. The student may be able to tolerate only one set of stimuli at a time.

- Be ready to curtail an activity that isn't working.

- Make directions as concrete as possible. Show pictures if you can.

- Rehearse situations which are out of routine, such as going to an assembly or a classroom party. Make expectations clear.

- Break down assignments into small isolated steps. When one step is mastered, go to the next step. Do not let unfinished assignments accumulate.

- Develop communication skills through spoken language, communication boards, sign language or any combination of these.

- Teach students who are mute to use augmentative communication devices, which may increase communication and social behavior and reduce problem behaviors.

- Use social stories in which a child is acting inappropriately and is taught to replace the poor behavior with appropriate behavior.

- Use video tapes with closed captioning to help teach reading.

- If the student is willing, make a game of attempting to make eye contact while the student swings on a swing.

- Capitalize on fixations by using them as rewards or transitions for learning. Do not try to remove them.

- Try to replace behaviors (hand flapping, rocking, etc.) with more appropriate behavior and forms of communication.

- Discourage inappropriate hugging in a way that is not rejecting.

- Try to replace acting-out and self-destructive behavior with other forms of communication.

- Use music or music therapy to help calm the student and reduce stimulating behavior.

- Demand, but do not always expect, age-appropriate behavior.

- Praise all successes.

- Provide opportunities for taking turns and sharing.

- Encourage and support choice-making.

- Use *emotion stickers* to help the student describe his feelings.

- Inform the librarian, lunch room staff and other school workers of the special characteristics and needs of the student.

- If the placement in your room is not working out, ask the administrator to call another staffing to alter the original plans or change the student's placement.

Suggestions for Handling an Outburst

- Because most outbursts are caused by the student's inability to communicate needs, work on improving communication skills.

- Do not feel that an occasional outburst makes a student unacceptable in a regular classroom. Students with autism can be taught to change their behavior.

- Consider having the student wear a weighted pressure vest to help him stay calm.

- Request training for yourself and your aid in approved methods for restraining a student having an outburst. Use this method when appropriate.

- With the help of the parents and the aid determine a plan to handle outbursts, particularly those that are physical. The plan should be aimed at helping the student regain control and should not be punitive. Establish when the plan should be implemented. Advise the student of the plan.

- Request the parents commit to picking up the student from school anytime the student becomes unable to control his behavior for the day.

- Try to determine the cause of the outbursts, especially if there are several, by asking the student or by trying to analyze the events preceding the outburst. If possible, remove the cause.

- If the student appears to be getting agitated over a classroom activity, give the student another activity or, if necessary, move the student to a safe place.

- If the student feels he is becoming upset and can express this, or if the teacher or aid feel the student is becoming upset, have the aid remove the student to a safe place. If the student is capable of writing what is bothering him, have him do so.

- Remove the student from outside stimulation.

- Calm the student with as little touching as possible.

- Do not allow the student to injure himself or any other person in the classroom. Use restraining as a last resort.

- Teach relaxation techniques to the student.

Glossary

Applied Behavior Analysis (ABA) – the idea that a certain behavior follows a certain stimulus; by controlling the environment you can control the behavior

Asperger's syndrome – a disorder, considered a milder form of autism, in which a person has many of the behaviors associated with autism but not the language delays or cognitive impairments

augmentative and alternate communication devices – communication boards which enable, in varying degrees, students with limited or no verbal communication to communicate

childhood disintegrative disorder – a pervasive developmental disorder in which a normally developing child suffers significant loss of previously acquired skills

echolalia –the parroting of words or phrases usually, but not necessarily, immediately after they are heard

echopraxia – the automatic and meaningless repetition of a movement which was previously observed

Landau-Kleffner Syndrome – a form of childhood epilepsy which disrupts the use of communication and often results in several autistic-type behaviors

motor disorder – a condition in which abnormal posture or movement is present

perseveration – persistent repetition of a verbal or motor response

pervasive developmental disorder – a disorder which impairs several facets of life including communication, behavior, social interactions and learning

pica – the persistent eating of non-food substances, primarily hair, finger nails, string, paint chips, etc.

Picture Exchange Communication System (PECS) – a communication system for children unable to speak that utilizes a book of pictures the child can point to

Rett's disorder – a progressive disorder, affecting only girls, in which a normally developing child loses previously acquired skills including use of hands, loss of speech, loss of motor control, and mental retardation

savant syndrome – the ability to memorize trivial facts or be able to perform unimportant mental tasks despite generally lower mental functioning

sensory integration disorder (also called *sensory processing disorder*) – a complex disorder of the brain causing people to misinterpret everyday sensory information

social stories – short stories that include situations in which a child is acting inappropriately and is taught to replace the poor behavior with appropriate behavior

stereotypical behavior – persistent repetition of an action or speech pattern

TEACCH (Treatment and Education of Communication Handicapped Children) – a program that uses various techniques applied to the underlying conditions of the environment to help autistic children learn

theory of mind – an impairment that prevents autistic children from understanding that other people have their own ideas, beliefs, intentions and desires

Reference Books

Fouse, Beth and Maria Wheeler. *A Treasure Chest of Behavioral Strategies for Individuals with Autism.* Arlington, TX: Future Horizons, 1997.

Gerlach, Elizabeth K. *Autism Treatment Guide*, 3rd ed. Arlington, TX: Future Horizons, 2003.

Kluth, Paula. *You're Going to Love This Kid!: Teaching Students with Autism in the Inclusive Classroom.* Baltimore, MD: Brookes Publishing Company, 2003.

Koegel, Robert L. and Lynn Kern Koegel, eds. *Teaching Children With Autism: Strategies for Initiating Positive Interactions and Improving Learning Opportunities.* Baltimore, MD: Brookes Publishing Company, 2003.

Stratton, Joyce and Phyllis Coyne, Carol Gray, Ann Fullerton, eds. *Higher Functioning Adolescents and Young Adults With Autism: A Teacher's Guide.* Austin, TX: PRO-ED, Inc., 1996.

Williams, Donna. *Autism: An Inside-Out Approach: An Innovative Look at the Mechanics of 'Autism' and Its Developmental 'Cousins.'* London, UK: Jessica Kingsley Publishers, 1996.

Web Sites

About.com
   www.autism.about.com

Autism Research Institute
   www.autism.com/ari

Autism Society of America
   www.autism-society.org

The Center for the Study of Autism
   www.autism.org

Cure Autism Now
   www.cureautismnow.org

Oceans of Emotions
   www.oceansofemotions.com

Chapter VI

Students with Mental Retardation

- *Students with Mild Mental Retardation*
- *Students with Moderate Mental Retardation*

Definition

Mental retardation refers to substantial limitations in present functioning. It is characterized by significantly subaverage intellectual functioning, existing concurrently with related limitations in two or more of the following applicable adaptive skill areas: communication, self-care, home living, social skills, community use, self-direction, health and safety, functional academics, leisure, and work. Mental retardation manifests before age 18.

—American Association on Mental Retardation

(Reprinted with permission of the American Association on Mental Retardation, 1992.)

Mental retardation is classified in a number of ways: by IQ, by performance or by the amount of support needed. The sub-categories below incorporate all three factors. Though some of the terms used are considered outdated, they are included because they are still in common use. The IQ ranges are merely a guide and should not be used as a sole factor in determining the level of mental retardation.

There are four sub-categories of mental retardation:

1. mild – IQ 50 to 70–75; educable mentally handicapped (EMH) or educable mental retardation (EMR); require intermittent support services in school, work and home living (includes about 85 percent of people with mental retardation);

2. moderate – IQ 35 to 50; trainable mentally handicapped (TMH) or trainable mentally retarded (TMR); require limited support services and supervision in school, work and home living (includes about 10 percent of people with mental retardation);

3. severe – IQ 20 to 35; require extensive support and supervision; and

4. profound – IQ under 20; require pervasive support and extensive care in all aspects of their lives.

This chapter discusses only students with mild or moderate retardation. Severe and profound retardation are included in Chapter XII – Students with Severe and Multiple Disabilities.

Important Facts about Students with Mental Retardation

• Mental retardation can be an entity unto itself or part of a syn-

76

drome. Some disorders which may have mental retardation as a component, but do not necessarily include it, are Down syndrome, fragile X syndrome, spina bifida, phenylketonuria (PKU), Tay-Sachs disease, cerebral palsy, galactosemia, hydrocephaly, microcephaly, Duchene muscular dystrophy, Turner syndrome, Klinefelter syndrome, Prader-Willi syndrome, fetal alcohol syndrome, Rett's disorder, Cornelia de Lange syndrome and Raye syndrome.

- Although many people picture a child with mental retardation as a Down syndrome person, most people with mental retardation have a normal appearance.

- Children with Down syndrome may also have hearing defects, congenital heart disease, intestinal abnormalities, eye problems, skeletal problems or thyroid dysfunction.

- Other than students with severe and multiple disabilities, students with mental retardation are the group least likely to be placed in the regular classroom.

- The term "mental retardation" cannot be the sole determinant of a student's ability. Students with mental retardation possess a wide range of abilities.

- Some parents cannot come to terms with their child's mental retardation and are likely to have guilt feelings about it. It should be remembered that no one is to blame (except in cases of prenatal substance and alcohol abuse) and attempts to place blame are destructive.

- The teacher should view the abilities of the student not the limitations.

- It should be decided at the staffing in which areas the student will be doing specialized classwork and which classwork will be done with the rest of the class.

- Students with mental retardation have personal interests and hobbies, which can be used to develop classroom activities for them.

- Students with mild and moderate mental retardation are aware they are not as smart as their classmates. It is important for the teacher to acknowledge their achievements and increase their self-esteem.

- The teacher should be sensitive to the feelings of the students with mental retardation, as they may not be able to express their feelings in words.

- The teacher may feel guilty about advancing to the next topic and leaving the student behind if the student with mental retardation is not grasping the concept. However, if both teacher and the student are trying hard, they should both feel successful about any progress that is made.

- The incidence of children born with mental retardation can be reduced if students are taught from junior high school and up the necessity of proper diet and medical care during pregnancy as well as the avoidance of drugs, alcohol and tobacco. Boys should learn this as well as girls.

Characteristics of
Students with Mild and Moderate Mental Retardation

- Possess limited social skills.

- Behave immaturely.

- Become frustrated easily.

- Lack self-confidence.

- Exhibit the need for a great amount of support.

- Tend to withdraw.

- Often forget self-maintenance and grooming tasks.

- Lack motivation.

- Are often sick and absent from school.

- Display some stereotypical behaviors.

- Lack age-appropriate language skills.

- Function substantially lower in academic work.

- Exhibit poor metacognitive skills.

- Are usually unable to think abstractly.

- Tend to oversimplify concepts.

- Tend to focus on a single aspect of a learning situation.

- May not be able to formulate learning strategies.

- Don't retain learning for long periods of time.

- Have short attention spans.

- Have difficulty in skill transference.

Suggestions for Working with a Student with Mild Mental Retardation

In general classroom procedures

- Include the student in all classroom activities.

- Assign classroom duties.

- Work at the student's skill level instead of the class' skill level.

- Try to keep assignments similar or related to what the rest of the class is doing.

- Give short assignments.

- Provide an outline of the lesson.

- Provide notes on the material.

- Allow the student to highlight passages in the textbook.

- Help the student keep books and papers organized.

- Work on the student's ability to pay attention for longer periods of time.

- Teach the student to start work without special prompts.

- When putting work on the board to be copied, make sure it is up long enough for the student to copy it.

- Teach keyboard skills and allow the student to work and play games on the computer.

- Avoid having the student work too long at one activity.

- Use repetition.

- Use mnemonics.

- Relate the class lesson to real-life experiences and skills.

- Use self-correcting workbooks and work sheets so the student can get immediate feedback without the embarrassment of always asking for help.

- Say the student's name to attract his attention before asking a question.

- Pair the student with a study-buddy.

- Praise frequently but only when earned.

- Review and practice real-life situations.

- Work on improving self-motivation, self-direction and choice-making skills.

- Enhance your verbal communication by using gestures, body language and intonation.

- Teach appropriate ways to express emotions.

- Work out a separate grading system with the school administration and the student's parents.

In language arts

- Develop writing skills.

- Teach the spelling of basic words.

- Improve handwriting.

- Improve reading skills and encourage reading for pleasure.

- Encourage silent reading.

- Stress language skills.

- Provide opportunities to speak in class.

In mathematics

- Work on the four operations with whole numbers. Use concrete examples and manipulatives.

- Teach calculator skills.

- Use real-life story problems.

- Teach money skills.

In social studies

- Teach awareness of the community and its services.

- Teach use of public transportation and getting around the community.

- Teach about the major political offices and how to vote.

In physical education

- Teach good eating habits.

- Teach personal maintenance skills and physical fitness.

- Develop gross and fine-motor skills.

- Insist on age-appropriate play at recess.

Suggestions for Working with a Student with Moderate Mental Retardation

In classroom procedures

- Ensure the goals set for the student are realistic.

- Request help from either the special education teacher or an aid.

- Develop plans with the parents so work can be reinforced at home.

- Provide a daily schedule. Use pictures if necessary.

- Give shorter and easier assignments than those given to the rest of the class.

- Break assignments into components. Allow additional time.

- Have the student repeat the directions.

- Have the student talk through working activity.

- Give concrete rather than abstract examples.

- Teach same or similar tasks in different environments and circumstances.

- Allow the student to answer aloud into a tape recorder.

- Use large print books.

- Provide the student with study sheets which require filling in blanks.

- Set up a system of rewards that allows the student to view his progress, such as a chart with stars awarded for each assignment completed.

- Change rewards frequently to keep the student interested.

- Help the student learn routines.

- Do not put student into too many situations where choices have to be made.

- Reduce distractions.

- Work on daily living skills (functional curriculum).

- Work on social skills.

- Develop the student's ability to pay attention.

- Develop the student's ability to become self-motivated.

- For group work, assign the student to a specific group and a specific role within the student's capabilities.

- Develop an alternative method of grading.

- Work on developing vocabulary and communication skills.

- Insist that classmates treat the student as an equal member of the class.

- Protect the student from being teased.

- Include the student in as many classroom activities as is possible.

- In a way that is not rejecting, discourage the student from hugging inappropriately.

In language arts

- Work on word attacks for reading.

- Work on building reading comprehension.

- Teach reading for information and pleasure.

- Increase spoken and written vocabulary.

- Help develop conversational skills.

- Develop vocabulary for describing feelings.

In mathematics

- Teach skills for shopping.

- Teach skills for managing personal finances.

- Teach how to tell time on both an analog and digital clock.

- Teach math skills needed for a job.

- Teach addition and subtraction using a number line. Gradually increase the length.

In social studies

- Teach about resources in the community and where to go for specific kinds of help.

- Teach about holidays and what they commemorate.

Additional Areas of Functional Curriculum for a Student with Mild or Moderate Mental Retardation

In job training

- Teach how to apply for a job and how to fill out a job application.

- Teach skills that will be needed on a job.

- Teach how to follow a work schedule.

- Teach how to cope with problems that arise on a job.

- Teach social skills for working with others.

In personal care

- Teach grooming.

- Teach personal hygiene, cleanliness and nutrition.

- Give instructions on what to do when ill.

- Teach about love relationships.

In independent living

- Give instructions for keeping a clean living environment.

- Teach how to shop for food.

- Teach how to prepare food.

- Teach how to use appliances and utilities in the home.
- Teach how to handle emergencies.

In community use

- Teach what shopping resources are in the community.
- Develop ability to use public transportation.
- Teach how to get help.

In leisure time

- Introduce the student to several leisure time activities.
- Help the student to develop appropriate relationships.

In behavior and social skills

- Demand age-appropriate behavior.
- Teach the student the rules of the room and insist they be followed.
- Develop a number of tasks the student can do in the classroom.
- Provide opportunities for the student to interact with classmates.
- Encourage the parents of classmates to invite the student to birthday parties, sleep-overs and other out-of-school activities.

Alternative Ways of Testing a Student with Mild or Moderate Mental Retardation

- Test-taking for students with mental retardation is an area of major adjustment. Some students may find tests threatening because they know they cannot do well. Others will feel ashamed because they are given a different test or are not being tested at all. The teacher has several options for testing:

  1. give the regular test,
  2. give the regular test but grade more generously,
  3. give the regular test orally one-on-one,
  4. give a shorter version of the test,
  5. allow the test to be taken at home,
  6. give an easier test on the same topic,
  7. give the test and allow the student to do it with the aid,

84

8. give additional time for taking the test,

9. give an alternate assignment instead of the test, and

10. give an open book test in which the emphasis is on finding the answers.

For a younger student, the teacher should choose the most appropriate option for the particular student. For an older student, the teacher can let the student pick two or three appropriate options.

- Some students may ask to take the same test that everyone else is taking. Although the student most likely cannot pass the test, the self-esteem gained in the attempt may outweigh the benefits of passing an easier test. In this situation the student should be praised for trying hard.

- Giving the student no test at all is a disservice to the student.

- Giving the entire class an easier test in an attempt to make the student with mental retardation feel better is a disservice to the entire class.

Glossary

anencephaly – a condition in which the brain is either absent or not completely developed

anoxia (also called *hypoxia*) – termination of oxygen flow to the brain causing the death of brain cells

authentic instruction – a teaching method that connects knowledge and skills to a student's everyday life situations

community-based instruction – a teaching method that uses a student's community setting to teach life skills

developmental disability – a mental or physical disability developed in childhood which is likely to be permanent

epicanthic fold – the flap of skin over the innermost corner of the eye that is characteristic of children with Down syndrome

functional curriculum – a curriculum which focuses on developing skills in communication, self-care, home living, community living, socialization and job skills

generalization – the ability to apply what is learned to other settings

hypoxia – (see *anoxia*)

job coach – a person who works on a job site helping employees with limited skills do the work and become integrated into the workplace

learned helplessness – a condition in which a person expects to fail and, instead of trying, learns to depend on someone else to do the job

life-skills curriculum – (see *functional curriculum*)

outer directedness – a condition in which students distrust their own solutions and seek answers from others

sheltered workshop – a facility which provides employment with close supervision for those employees who are unable to work well independently

stereotypical behavior – persistent repetition of an action or speech pattern

task analysis – the breaking down of complicated complex tasks into smaller components that are easier to learn

trisomy 21 – the most common cause of Down syndrome, which indicates a third chromosome attached to the twenty-first gene pair

Reference Books

Ainsworth, Patricia and Pamela C. Baker. *Understanding Mental Retardation*. Jackson, MS: University Press of Mississippi, 2004.

Cronin, Mary E. and James R. Patton. *Life Skills Instruction for All Students With Special Needs: A Practical Guide for Integrating Real-Life Content into the Curriculum*. Austin, TX: PRO-ED, Inc., 1993.

Edwards, Jean and David Dawson. *My Friend David: A Source Book About Down's Syndrome and a Personal Story About Friendship*. Austin, TX: PRO-ED, Inc., 1983.

Guralnick, Michael J., ed. *The Effectiveness of Early Intervention*. Baltimore, MD: Brookes Publishing Company, 1997.

Wehmeyer, Michael J. et al. *Teaching Students with Mental Retardation*. Baltimore, MD: Brookes Publishing Company, 2002.

Web Sites

The American Association on Mental Retardation
www.aamr.org

The Arc
www.thearc.org

The National Down Syndrome Society
www.ndss.org

Chapter VII

Students with Giftedness and Talents

- *Students with Giftedness*
- *Students with Talents*

Definitions

The term "gifted and talented" when used in respect to students, children or youth means students, children or youth who give evidence of high performance capability in areas such as intellectual, creative, artistic, or leadership ability, or in specific academic fields, and who require service or activities not ordinarily provided by the school in order to fully develop such abilities.

—Public Law 103-382 – Title XIV (1988)

Giftedness and talent is an overlapping of above average ability, creativity and task commitment brought to bear upon general or specific performance areas.

—J. S. Renzulli

(Reprinted with permission from *Phi Delta Kappan*, Vol. 60, No. 3, p.180. Copyright 1978 Joseph S. Renzulli.)

Though it can be argued that every student is gifted or talented in some way, this chapter will discuss only those who are exceptionally gifted and talented, using the following terms:

1. *giftedness* – high intellectual ability and an IQ at least two standard deviations above the norm (the 130 to 135 range);
2. *talents* – unusually high ability in athletics, leadership or the arts.

Important Facts about
Students with Giftedness and Talents

- Students who are gifted and talented usually find the regular classroom to be limiting. They are capable of going far beyond their peers. The regular classroom cannot provide them with the learning opportunities they need to maximize their abilities. This is what makes them special education students.

- Students who are gifted and talented are the only group of special education students who do not have federally mandated programs. The federal government encourages the states to set up programs for them, but the final decision is left with the school districts and the states, who base their decisions on the availability of revenue and the pressures of local activists.

90

- Because there is no mandated programming for either identifying or providing for students with giftedness, it is incumbent on the regular classroom teacher to meet this need.

- The motivation and performance of a student with giftedness declines in the absence of mental stimulation.

- Gifted and talented programs are often lacking due to the prevailing attitude that bright students can take care of themselves and are least in need of special programs. Though this may be true, the philosophy of American education is that each student be given the opportunity to reach his or her limits of ability. Therefore, a lack of gifted programs does not meet this philosophy.

- Every American high school has at least two programs for the gifted and talented—the boys' football team and the boys' basketball team. It is not wrong to have these programs, but it is wrong to have only these programs.

- American educators are often critical of the fact that other industrial nations do not pay enough attention to their most difficult students. Americans, however, don't pay enough attention to their most productive students.

Students with Giftedness

Definition

Giftedness is a combination of greater awareness, greater sensitivity, and greater ability to understand and transform perceptions into intellectual and emotional experience.

—Annemarie Roeper

(Reprinted with permission from *The Roeper Review*, November, 1982, Vol. 5, No.2, p.8-10. Copyright 1982 The Roeper Review.)

Important Facts about Students with Giftedness

- Statistically only one person in one thousand has an IQ of 137 or higher, and only one person in one million has an IQ of 160 or higher.

- Many districts do not have programs for students with giftedness. The responsibility then falls on the shoulders of the classroom teacher. In the worst case scenario, the classroom teacher does nothing to meet the special needs of the students with giftedness. In the second worse case scenario, the classroom teacher tries to supply an appropriate program for the students with giftedness all by herself.

- A good student should not be confused with a student with giftedness. The student with giftedness may or may not be a good student. The good student will consistently do good work, but the student with giftedness has the potential to produce concepts, ideas, programs and projects. If the teacher can meet the needs of this student, there is a good chance the potential can be reached.

- Good students process information in a linear manner but do it faster and better than average students. They still need to practice the new skill for mastery. Students with giftedness process information in divergent ways and master it immediately.

- Americans generally have a love-hate relationship with the gifted. They enjoy knowing about exceptionally brilliant people, but don't appreciate them personally and often resent them.

- Parents and teachers of the students with giftedness sometimes push them into performing to show off their ability. This may not be good for the student.

- Gifted girls often have difficulty displaying their intelligence. They are frequently taught it is not good to be too smart, because people won't like them and boys won't ask them out on dates. They learn it is better to be quiet and keep their gifts to themselves.

- Gifted boys are more likely than gifted girls to be placed in special programs, receive one-on-one help and encouragement, and receive additional services. This happens with both male and female teachers.

- Americans put a great deal of emphasis on IQ scores. IQ scores merely predict a student's capabilities in school. Some schools use IQ scores as the sole determinant for getting into special programs; others refuse to use them at all.

- Students with giftedness are not gifted in all areas.

- Students with giftedness are capable of seeing the world in different terms than their classmates and even their teachers. They tend to see people and events in a more integrated and more dynamic way and are able to view the future as well as focus on the present.

• The belief that people with giftedness are prone to emotional problems is a myth. On the contrary, people with giftedness have a better chance of finding healthy ways to cope in life than average people. Their often nonconformist thinking and behavior may cause others to consider them unusual or eccentric, but they are seldom harmful or destructive.

• Teachers will sometimes become overly concerned with the social adjustment of a student with giftedness and insist the student partake in social situations. However, students with giftedness often prefer to focus on academics and should not be forced to sacrifice them to develop social skills.

• Teachers receiving a student with giftedness frequently expect a model student and are disappointed to find the student is more often challenging and demanding. If the teacher meets these challenges and demands, she may have a model student. However, if the teacher tries to force the student to conform to the rest of the class, the student will quickly become oppositional and disruptive, and the teacher will find she has a highly skilled adversary.

• Gifted children are more often found in upper and middle class neighborhoods than in working class neighborhoods because:

1. high academic ability may be more highly regarded in upper and middle class neighborhoods than in working class neighborhoods,

2. middle and upper class families are more likely to nurture giftedness and have resources to do so,

3. schools in upper and middle class neighborhoods have higher expectations for their students, and

4. students in working class neighborhoods are more likely to hide their giftedness from their peers.

• There are students who are both gifted and learning disabled. Teachers need to watch for flashes of intelligence in a seemingly average student, which may indicate a learning disability masking intelligence and intelligence masking a learning disability.

Characteristics of Students with Giftedness

- Accomplish grade-appropriate work with ease.
- Have a mature vocabulary.
- View learning with pleasure.
- May slide along just to get by with work but will not forsake interest in learning.
- Are always creative, inventive and filled with ideas.
- Are always highly curious.
- Have a propensity to organize information.
- Usually emerge as the organizer and the leader of a group.
- Have a good memory.
- Become deeply involved.
- Look for additional work.
- Are intense.
- Have the ability to do abstract thinking.
- Can evaluate what has just been learned.
- Understand the interrelatedness of knowledge.
- Understand the relationship between themselves and the world.
- Have the ability to see a problem from more than one side.
- Have the ability to produce multiple solutions.
- Have a broad understanding of problems.
- Are energetic in attacking problems.
- Can provide rational explanations in all areas.
- Have assuredness about solutions.
- Are modest about their accomplishments.
- Take it for granted that they are correct.
- Have the ability to generate more questions.
- Have preference for conversing with older people.

- May prefer books or computers to friends.

- Spend large amounts of time with other students with giftedness.

- Are unusually sensitive to others.

- Have a strong sense of fairness and justice.

- Are very critical of themselves and often have feelings of frustration.

- Gauge their achievements not on those of their classmates but on their own set of expectations.

Suggestions for Working with a Student with Giftedness

- Do not be intimidated by a child with a high IQ. A 10-year-old child with an IQ of 150 has the mental intelligence of a 15-year-old but the general knowledge and life experience of a 10-year-old.

- Teach the student the value of his gift.

- Teach the rest of the class to value the gift of the student.

- Be flexible. Teaching a student with giftedness can be a good learning experience for both the teacher and the student.

- Keep expectations high.

- Emphasize the use of knowledge rather than just the acquisition of it.

- When working in groups, place bright students in the same group to provide a more challenging environment.

- Arrange for the student to take some classes with older students in higher grades.

- Consider clustering high ability students of various ages in one group.

- If any faculty member has a skill in an area of strength of the student with giftedness, see if a connection can be made with that teacher and the student with giftedness.

- Develop creative thinking, critical thinking and problem solving.

- With the parents look for out-of-school programs and opportunities in the community where the student can apply and expand her skills.

- Arrange the room in a way that invites inquiry with books on many subjects, objects of interest in several areas, and a variety of materials. Encourage exploration of encyclopedias and other reference works.

- Encourage the student to enter competitions.

- Incorporate the student's areas of expertise into other areas of study.

- Compress more than one year's work into the year.

- Use stimulating "what if" questions, which can be answered orally or in an essay.

- Avoid holding back pertinent work because it is supposed to be done next year.

- Do not push the student ahead too hard or too fast. Be aware of resistance.

- Allow students who gain free time by finishing work early to do extra work in their area of expertise or interest.

- Give the student projects rather than individual assignments (i.e., if each student is learning about an individual European country, have the student with giftedness devise her own project with European geography).

- Assign projects in which data is gathered and presented, conclusions are drawn, concepts are formed and information is analyzed and evaluated.

- Stimulate creativity by providing opportunities to write, draw, dance, act, engage in music, etc.

- When developing his own project, have the student work from raw data rather than the materials of others. This allows him to analyze and synthesize rather than summarize and record.

- Reduce the amount of drill for accuracy (i.e., if the class is practicing multiplication, have the student do the first 5 to show understanding and the last 10 to show mastery).

- Give permission to freely use the library and other reference rooms.

- Avoid giving inappropriate work to a student. Although it is easy to say that it won't hurt a student with giftedness to do work that is too easy, in fact it wastes the student's school time.

- If the student with giftedness completes the work early, give additional work that is more difficult than that just completed.

- Do not become upset or demanding if the student uses a different way of doing the work you taught. If the student's way is not good, it will be discovered.

- Do not make the student with giftedness the junior teacher or tutor. Many students with giftedness do not like this kind of work nor should they be expected to.

- Do not insist the student work on exercises which have no value to her.

- Do not push the student in a particular direction.

- Do not force social skills on the student. Do not be concerned if social life becomes neglected in favor of academic life.

- Do not assume the student's emotional maturity matches his intellectual maturity.

- Do not assume the student has leadership abilities.

- Allow the student to engage in age-appropriate activities.

- Be sensitive to any feelings of isolation or loneliness the student might develop.

- Promote extracurricular activities in your school.

- Promote programs for the gifted in your district.

Students with Talents

Definition

The talented are those who excel in human endeavors. Though "talented" is a term often used interchangeably with "gifted," this text uses the term to describe those students who possess a high level of ability in non-academic areas.

Important Facts about Students with Talents

- Students who are talented have a need to develop their talents. The school has a duty to provide for this. A young athlete should

97

not be held back from participating in sports because of poor performance in algebra any more than a budding mathematician should be held back from algebra because of poor performance in gym.

Characteristics of Students with Talents

- Possess a skill level surpassing those of their peer groups.
- Spend an inordinate amount of time in their area of expertise.
- Often lose track of time when engaged in their field.
- Engage in their field for love of it rather than the promise of any reward.
- Interested and informed about other people in their field of interest.

Suggestions for Working with a Student with Talents

- Support the student's pursuit of excellence.
- Ask the class to support the student by attending events in which the student is participating.
- Provide the student with biographies of people in his area of expertise, so he can see how other people have handled this talent.
- Allow the student to take some classes with another teacher who has the same or a similar talent.
- Allow the student to incorporate talents with other classwork.
- Help the student select school activities and community programs that will enhance the skill.
- Be flexible with the student's schedule to allow the student time to participate in activities.
- Do not push the student too hard or too fast.
- Do not make participation in pursuit of the talent a reward or punishment.
- Do not make the student feel the area of talent is not as important as other types of schoolwork.

Glossary

acceleration – presenting curriculum in a shorter period of time

cluster grouping – placing students with a similar talent, gift or interest in the same group so they can follow their pursuit together

compacting – reducing the amount of standard work and replacing it with enrichment work

conceptualization – the ability to formulate original ideas

convergent thinking – reaching a conclusion through known facts and thinking skills such as memory and reason

creativity – a type of intelligence marked by divergent thought bringing forth original ideas

differentiated curriculum – a curriculum which is flexible to allow independent and accelerated learning

divergent thinking – reaching a conclusion through creativity, flexibility and originality

enrichment – adding material to a topic to give it greater breadth and depth

intelligence quotient (IQ) – mental age (MA) divided by chronological age (CA) and multiplying by 100. The result is an indication of how likely a person is to do well in school. Average range is considered 90 to 110. An IQ of 160 or higher is generally considered "genius."

magnet school – a specialized school which brings together students who wish to pursue a common curriculum

telescoping – exploring a topic more deeply

webbing – a graphic representation of ideas and the relationships among them

Reference Books

Colangelo, Nicholas and Gary A. Davis. *Handbook of Gifted Education*. 3rd ed. Boston, MA: Allyn & Bacon, 2002.

Smutny, Joan Franklin et al. *Teaching Young Gifted Children in the Regular Classroom: Identifying, Nurturing, and Challenging Ages 4–9*. Minneapolis, MN: Free Spirit Publishing, 1997.

Strip, Carol Ann and Gretchen Hall. *Helping Gifted Children Soar: A Practical Guide for Parents and Teachers.* Scottsdale, AZ: Great Potential Press, 2000.

Winebrenner, Susan and Pamela Espeland. *Teaching Gifted Kids in the Regular Classroom: Strategies and Techniques Every Teacher Can Use to Meet the Academic Needs of the Gifted and Talented.* Minneapolis, MN: Free Spirit Publishing, 2000.

Winner, Ellen. *Gifted Children: Myths and Realities.* New York, NY: Basic Books, 1997.

Web Sites

Center for Talent Development at Northwestern University
www.ctd.northwestern.edu

Challenging Gifted Children in the Classroom
www.kidsource.com

Differentiating Curriculum
www.ericfacility.net

Internet Magazine for Gifted
www.mamamedia.com

National Association for Gifted Children
www.nagc.org

Chapter VIII

Students with Communication Disorders

Definition

Communication disorders are disturbances in normal speech and language that disrupt the communication process sufficiently to interfere with the transference of ideas. Communication disorders may be speech disorders, which are problems in creating speech orally, or language disorders, which are problems in receiving, understanding or formulating ideas and information.

Types of communication disorders:

I. *Speech disorders* – difficulties performing the neuromuscular movements of speech, most commonly articulation disorders

   A. *Articulation problems* – problems in producing words

   1. *Substitutions* – th for s, f for th, w for r. etc. (He lost his fwont toof.)
   2. *Omissions* – sounds left out of words (Gi' me a han'.)
   3. *Additions* – extra sounds added to words (Stop pushering me.)
   4. *Distortions* – using the wrong sound in a word formation ("nes" for "yes."

   B. *Fluency problems* – problems with the even flow of language production

   1. *Stuttering* – an unwanted repetition of sound within a word (G-g-g-get me out of he-e-e-ear.)
   2. *Stammering* – long pause between words, sometimes filled with repeated use of one of the words in the sentence or a meaningless sound (And, and, and, and then we uh, uh, uh, urr went to bed.)

   C. *Voice disorders* – qualities that make the speaker unpleasant to listen to

   1. *Disorders of volume* – vocal quality is too loud or too soft
   2. *Disorders of pitch* – vocal quality is too high or (rarely) too low
   3. *Disorders of quality* – vocal quality is too nasal, too breathy, whining, shrill or hoarse.

II. *Language disorders* – impairments in the ability to understand and/or use words in context both verbally and non-verbally

A. *Phonology* – the sequence of sounds in a word—incorrect sequence ("fatser" for "faster") or the wrong sound ("falser" for "faster")

B. *Morphology* – the way sounds are combined to make meaningful words (boy + s makes plural "boys", want + ed makes past tense "wanted")

C. *Syntax* – the order of words in a sentence (Cookie I want.)

D. *Semantics* – the substance, meaning and relationship between words to determine meaning of a phrase or sentence (You can bank on my bank shot.)

E. *Pragmatics* – communication in the social context, i.e., eye contact, body language, knowing when it is your turn to speak, using vocabulary appropriate to the occasion, understanding facial cues and nuances of voice

Problems which may have a psychological basis:

I. *Late talking and language delay*

A. *Late talking* – lack of speech or inappropriate speech for age level with inadequate comprehension, usually not affecting play with peers or pretend play (usually temporary)

B. *Language delay* – a lagging ability to communicate in speech and comprehension, usually accompanied gestures that are difficult to interpret

II. *Selective muteness* (previously called *elective muteness*) – a condition in which children who are perfectly capable of talking either stop talking altogether or stop talking to selected individuals (usually adults). Such children are usually between 4 and 8 years old; have tendencies towards anxiety, depression and dependency; are more commonly girls than in boys; and meet the diagnostic criteria for social phobia.

Communication problems that are not communication disorders:

Variations in language models – any accent or dialect which deviates from standard American English in vocabulary (I'm hangin' wi' my homey.), pronunciation (Vat you vant frum

103

me?), sentence structure (You want, maybe, I should go?), or use of individual words (this singer is really "bad"). Ebonics, a variation used by working-class African Americans, is the most discussed of these variations.

Important Facts about
Students with Communication Disorders

• Language disorders are more serious than speech disorders.

• The ability to communicate is probably the most important skill humans learn.

• Every classroom teacher should be concerned with developing their students' ability to communicate.

• Just as a teacher has every student read aloud to gauge each student's reading ability, so should a teacher have every student speak aloud to gauge each student's speech development.

• Most students with communication disorders spend all of or most of their day in the regular classroom.

• The two main concerns for the regular classroom teacher who has a student with a communication disorder are: (1) can the student understand what is being taught, and (2) can the student express what is being learned.

• Students who have difficulty expressing themselves because of a communication disorder will have some days when they can express themselves better than other days.

• Students can have problems with either their understanding or their ability to speak.

• Some communication problems can be solved with practice.

• Some speech disorders are the result of another disability such as cerebral palsy, multiple sclerosis, autism, mental retardation or a cleft palate.

• Students with serious speech disorders, including those who stutter, are less likely to be chosen by peers as social partners.

• Some young students have developmental stuttering because they are thinking faster than they can talk. Problems that are developmental, as opposed to physiological, are easier to resolve and may disappear as the child matures.

• Stuttering is not caused by nervousness. On the contrary, it causes nervousness in the speaker.

Characteristics of Students with both Speech and Language Disorders

• Continue to mispronounce words after having been corrected.

• Are often misunderstood by teachers and other students.

• Seldom speak in class.

Characteristics of Students with Speech Disorders

• Display unpleasant vocal characteristics.

• Exhibit a pronounced variation in speech.

• Omit first or last sounds of words.

• Display an unnatural flow of words with extensive pauses.

Characteristics of Students with Language Disorders

• Have trouble expressing ideas.

• Use extensive gestures and hand signals to replace words.

• Use vocabulary that is less than age appropriate.

• Use incorrect grammatical patterns.

• Often confuse pronouns.

• Use pronouns when nouns should be used.

• Have difficulty forming sentences.

• Omit words from sentences.

• Incorrectly sequence words within a sentence.

• Exhibit similar difficulties in both reading and writing.

• Misunderstand directions, often without asking for clarification.

Suggestions for Working with a Student with Communication Disorders

- With the help of your speech therapist, decide which of the following options would be most effective for the student:

  1. direct services from the speech therapist in a separate room,

  2. integrated services from the therapist in the regular classroom,

  3. collaborative services – the teacher and speech therapist work together, or

  4. consulting services – the speech therapist is a resource, or

  5. outside services.

- Be patient and accepting.

- Tell the student you understand the problem.

- Model good language usage. Avoid slang and using the vernacular.

- Model good listening skills by using head nods, eye contact, forward leaning posture, and brief responses.

- Work with the student on building vocabulary. If you use a vocabulary workbook, reinforce the words of the lessons in other subjects and general classroom conversation. Do not feel reluctant to use new words, even if they seem difficult. Children, especially the very young, have great capacity for learning new words.

- Make a point of having short conversations with a problem speaker. Talk about a subject that is of interest to the student.

- Try to have every student answer at least one question a day.

- When calling on a student to answer a question, say the student's name before you ask the question so he has time to prepare an answer.

- Children with communication disorders often need more time to formulate a response. Ask questions that can be answered by several students so the student has some time to plan a response.

- Present the student with choices that have to be made and expressed.

- Enunciate so the student can hear words pronounced correctly.

- Discuss the meaning of facial expressions and body language.

- If a student speaks a word incorrectly, repeat the phrase using the word correctly. (e.g., If the student says, "I want to go fatser", you say, "You want to go faster?")

- Model enhanced speaking. If a child says "I need paper," respond, "Do you need a sheet of paper for your writing assignment?"

- Encourage poor speakers to talk. Engage them in conversation whenever possible. Set up situations where they have to speak to you—give them too few supplies so they have to ask you for more, or put their boots or mittens on the wrong foot or hand so they have to correct you.

- Help the student have conversations with other students by having the students work in groups of threes or fours.

- Have the student practice oral reading with a partner, taking turns listening to each other.

- Have the class do choral reading.

- Have the students give prepared speeches in front of the class, even if they are less than a minute long. If the student is uncomfortable giving a speech, do not insist upon it.

- Ask the student if he would like to be called upon in class. Tell the student what question you are going to ask him tomorrow so he has a chance to rehearse his answer. Call on him only if he raises his hand when the question is asked.

- Call on reluctant speakers, especially when the desired response is only one or two words long.

- If you feel a speech problem can be helped with a minimal amount of work, keep the student back from lunch or at the end of the day for a few minutes to work on the problem.

- If you feel the student has made a mistake due to faulty learning, it is all right to correct the speaker. However, be careful not to over-correct to a point where the student no longer wants to talk in class.

- If the student has a problem with pitch or volume, ask the student in private if she would like you to work on the problem with you. If the student agrees, you can work out a private signal to let her know when she is not speaking in a desirable way.

- Do not call attention to a speech problem in front of the class.

- Do not allow a student with a speech problem to be teased by the other students.

- Maintain a safe environment for all students to practice their skills.

- Do not imitate a student to show how he sounds.

- Do not tape-record a student without his permission.

- Do not force a student to speak or read in front of the class if he strongly resists.

Suggestions for Working with a Student Who Stutters

- Do not respond to a stuttering student by *(a)* appearing impatient, *(b)* threatening punishment, *(c)* finishing the student's words or sentences, *(c)* telling the student to slow down, *(d)* telling the student to take a deep breath and start over, or *(e)* telling the student you won't call on him anymore.

- Capitalize on good days, when the child is not stuttering badly, by calling on the student for answers.

- Encourage the parents of stuttering students to have a relaxed home environment when the child is talking.

Suggestions for Working with a Student Who Speaks in a Variation of Standard English or in a Foreign Language

- Ask older students if they wish to work on Standard English skills. If so, work with them to achieve this goal.

- Do not make negative comments about another language or language variation.

- Do not demand that the student stop speaking a foreign language either in or out of class.

- Do not show disrespect for the way a student speaks.

- Decide if your school should develop a program for encouraging and helping students speak mainstream English.

Glossary

aphasia – partial or total loss of speech

apraxia – an injury to the brain in which ways of forming speech is forgotten

articulation – the ability to speak

cleft palate – a split in the upper part of the oral cavity, which causes nasality when speaking

developmental articulation disorder – trouble controlling the rate of speech

developmental expressive language disorder – trouble expressing one's thoughts

developmental receptive language disorder – trouble understanding what one hears

dialect – a regional or cultural variation of a language

Ebonics – a variation of Standard English most often spoken by working class African-Americans

elective mutism – see *selective mutism*

fluency – the quality of speaking with normal rhythms, patterns and speed

functional disorder – a disorder for which there is no known organic cause

grammar – the study of the choice and placement of words in sentences

hypernasality – vocal sounds made with too much air coming through the nose and not enough through the mouth

hyponasality – vocal sounds made with too much sound coming through the mouth and not enough through the nose

metalinguistic awareness – the ability to think critically about your speaking

morpheme – the smallest meaningful unit of speech

109

morphology – the rules that dictate how morphemes will be used to form words

organic disorder – a disorder caused by a neuromuscular mechanism problem

phonemes – the different sounds in a language

phonology – the rules that dictate how language is used in interactions among people

pitch – the quality of highness or lowness of sound based on the number of vibrations per second

pragmatics – using communication in its social context; this includes non-verbal communication

resonance – the quality of the sound of the voice

selective mutism – a disability associated with anxiety and social phobias in which a person (usually a child) voluntarily stops talking to one or more people

semantics – the rules which dictate how words are used meaningfully

syntax – the rules which dictate the order of words in a sentence

volume – the quality of loudness in a sound or voice

Reference Books

Adler, S. *Oral Communication Problems in Children and Adolescents*. Philadelphia, PA: Crane and Stratton, 1998.

Costello, J., and A. Holland. *Handbook of Speech and Language Disorders*. San Diego, CA: College Hill Press, 1986.

Hedge, M.N. *Introduction to Communication Disorders*, 3rd ed. Austin, TX: PRO-ED, 2001.

Warren, S.F. *Enhancing Children's Communication*. Baltimore, MD: Brookes Publishing Company, 1993.

Web Sites

American Speech-Language-Hearing Association (ASHA)
www.asha.org

Centre for Inclusive Education (Center for Communicative and Cognitive Disabilities)
www.edu.uwo.ca/cccd

Speech Pathology.com
www.speechpathology.com

Stuttering Foundation of America
www.stutterSFA.org

The Unicorn Children's Foundation
www.unicorn.com

Chapter IX

Students with Partial Hearing Loss and Deafness

- *Students with Partial Hearing Loss*
- *Students with Deafness*

Definitions

Hearing impairment [partial hearing loss] is an impairment in hearing whether permanent or fluctuating, that adversely affects a child's educational performance but which is not included under the definition of deafness.

—IDEA

Deafness is hearing impairment that is so severe that the child is impaired in processing linguistic information through hearing, with or without amplification, that adversely affects a child's educational performance.

—IDEA

Important Facts about
Students with Partial Hearing Loss and Deafness

- Many people with hearing loss object to the term "hearing impaired." They feel it implies something lacking or something wrong with them. They see themselves as a separate culture with its own language and prefer to use the terms "deaf" and "people with hearing loss."

- Hearing problems can be problems of loudness, pitch, clarity or with sound interference, such as tinnitus.

- Some diseases that may cause hearing loss and deafness are otitis media (middle ear infection), rubella, meningitis, premature birth, mother-child RH incompatibility and cytomegalovirus (CMV). Hereditary and genetic factors may also be causes.

- Severity of hearing loss is determined by the amount of decibels the person is unable to hear. The following scale is used:

  can't hear 15–40 db----------mild loss

  can't hear 40–65 db----------moderate loss

  can't hear 65–90 db----------severe loss

  can't hear 90 db + ------------profound loss

  (The last two groups are considered deaf.)

- About 30 percent of children with hearing loss also have

another disability.

- In the past the average age of diagnosing a child with congenital hearing loss was 30 months, resulting in a long delay in teaching language skills. Current devices now test for hearing loss a few days after birth, providing the opportunity for language skills to be taught at an earlier age.

- Children with sensorineural hearing loss can have partial hearing restored with a cochlear implant. This procedure produces varying degrees of success. The deaf community does not support the procedure because they feel the deaf culture is a rich culture, which people do not have to leave by way of a surgical procedure.

- Hearing loss alone has no effect on intelligence.

- Hearing aids can only restore volume. They cannot restore clarity. Wearing a hearing aid to compensate for hearing loss is not at all similar to wearing eyeglasses to compensate for vision loss.

- American Sign Language (ASL) is not a translation of English into signs. It is a unique language with its own rules and syntax. For many people in the deaf culture it is their primary language.

- To ensure that a child learns ASL it should be taught to the child before age six. The children who are successful in learning ASL do better academically and have fewer behavior problems than those who struggle with it.

- In working with students with hearing loss the primary concern is to teach communication skills. Students with deafness have a difficult time learning spoken language. Therefore, they are often behind in reading skills and other academics in which reading is required.

- About 90 percent of children with deafness have hearing parents.

- Some parents of children with hearing loss never learn to communicate manually with their children.

Characteristics of
Students with Partial Hearing Loss and Deafness

- Routinely lag behind hearing students with similar intelligence in attaining communication skills. (This is particularly true among those with prelingual hearing loss.)

- Often become isolated or may isolate themselves from their hearing classmates.

- May develop psychological problems because their hearing parents may have difficulty bonding with a deaf child.

- May be embarrassed by their loss or by the way they speak.

- May have problems adjusting to a hearing society.

Characteristics of Students with Undiagnosed Hearing Loss

- Have limited vocabulary.

- Lack proper speech development.

- Speak unclearly.

- Speak with unusual intonation.

- Stare at people's lips when they are speaking.

- Cock head or turn head to one side when listening.

- Ask classmates to repeat instructions just given.

- Ask a lot of questions about material or directions just given.

- Withdraw from oral activities.

- Work best in small groups.

- Engage in either acting-out or withdrawn behavior.

Suggestions for Working with a Student with Partial Hearing Loss

- Seat the student in the front of the room. If the student has unilateral hearing loss assign a seat in which the student's better ear is nearer to the teacher.

- If the student uses a hearing aid make sure it is in working order. Ask the parents for a supply of extra batteries.

- Make sure the classroom is well lit, so the student can see clearly to lip-read.

- Improve the acoustics by installing carpets or rugs.

- Cut down on background noise by keeping windows closed in noisy neighborhoods and air conditioners low during oral presentations.

- If available, equip the student's desk with small speakers and wear a lapel mike.

- Whenever possible, arrange the seats in either a circle or semi-circle to allow the student greater access to what is being said.

- Use visual aids whenever possible.

- Write important notes on the chalkboard.

- Allow the student to tape-record the lectures and class discussions.

- Assign student helpers to assist the student with taking notes and completing other activities that would clarify the classwork.

- Speak within 10 feet of a student who is wearing a hearing aid.

- Face the class when speaking so the student can watch your lips. Be careful not to speak when you are writing on the chalkboard with your back to the class.

- Do not hold objects or your hands in front of your mouth when talking.

- If you have a large moustache consider a shave or a trim so your lips can be seen.

- Enunciate clearly.

- If the student is having trouble understanding you, try rephrasing and slowing down. To ensure the student's correct understanding, request that your instructions be repeated. If the student is still having difficulty, ask what you can do to be better understood.

- Arrange the day's learning schedule so there are periodic breaks from having to listen.

- Encourage the student to speak. If possible, help develop proper pronunciation.

- Include the student in choral readings and class skits.

- Look for deficits in the student's social skills and provide training.

Suggestions for Working with a Student with Deafness

- Seat the student in the front of the room so he can see you speaking.

- During class discussions have the student who is talking stand so the student with deafness can watch the speaker's lips.

- Assign a classmate each day to be the student's study-buddy. This person would help the student understand what is happening in the room, assist in note-taking and inform the student of any need to move from one place to another.

- Learn a few basic phrases in sign language and have the student teach them to the entire class.

- Give the student an advanced copy of the day's agenda.

- Give the student an outline of the lessons.

- Review the vocabulary for the lesson and give the student an advanced copy.

- Highlight important information in the text and study guides.

- Have the student read ahead so he will know the details of the topic as well as the vocabulary.

- Ask the student with deafness to write new information. This should be checked as there is often a difference between what the student understands in sign language and what he can express in English.

- Encourage a student who communicates in ASL to read to develop her ability to use English.

- Do not assume the student does not want to participate in music class. If possible give the student a choice of going or doing something else.

- Encourage the use of computers and educational computer programs so the student can get additional learning without having to listen. Teach keyboard skills.

- Use videotapes and slides that have printed captions.

- Encourage the student to speak, unless you have been instructed not to by the parents or a school administrator.

- Tell the student how he sounds. Make comments about pitch, speed, volume, intonation, pronunciation, etc.

- If it would be helpful, recommend speech therapy.

- Help the student to become socially involved with other students. Make sure the student with deafness knows the names of the other students.

- Do not fear using words such as "listen" or "hear."

- Make sure the student understands relevant messages received over the intercom.

- Work closely with the parents to make sure they are reinforcing at home the work being taught at school.

Suggestions for Working with a Sign Language Interpreter

- Expect that you may get a cluster of students with hearing loss in your classroom if a sign language interpreter is hired. It is usual and cost effective to have as many students as can be accommodated serviced by a single interpreter.

- Keep in mind that you are in charge of the learning. Before the sign language interpreter begins working in your classroom, discuss room procedures that will be changed by the presence of an additional adult.

- At the end of the day, discuss with the interpreter the next day's lessons. Make sure the interpreter understands the concepts which are to be taught.

- Give vocabulary to the sign language interpreter in advance so it can be taught to the student before the lesson.

- Be aware that there are a few seconds lag time between what is being said and what the student saw the interpreter communicate.

- Because the student may have difficulty watching your demonstration and the interpreter's signing at the same time, position yourselves so the student can view both of you simultaneously.

- When speaking to the student do not look at the interpreter. Look at the student as you would look at any other student to whom you were speaking. The interpreter will encode the message so the student can understand it. Allow the interpreter enough time to do this.

• It is all right for the sign language interpreter to work with other students if the primary responsibility remains with the student with hearing loss.

• Give rest periods to the speech language interpreter.

Methods of Communication Used by the Deaf

American Sign Language (ASL) – a visual gestural language indigenous to the American deaf community, which is not sign code for English but a unique language with its own syntax and grammar (often acquired as a first language by children with deafness who have deaf parents)

cued speech – a language method that uses coded hand shapes on the side of the face to supplement the sounds used in speech

fingerspell – a manual code technique with a configuration for each letter of the alphabet allowing words to be spelled letter by letter (good for conveying proper nouns and unusual words but slow when used to convey entire thoughts)

manually coded English (MCE) – a visual manually-spoken code with several variations that represents English (preferred by many teachers because its close relationship to English makes it easier for students to learn English)

oral / aural method – a communication technique that stresses the use of speech, hearing aids, voice, and speech reading skills to help children with deafness function in a talking society

The Rochester Method – a technique that uses fingerspell as words are simultaneously spoken

simultaneous communication – a technique of communication involving the use of sign language, fingerspelling, speech reading, sound amplification, and residual hearing

speech reading – the technique of watching people's lip movements and body language to understand meaning

total communication – the technique of speaking and signing simultaneously

Glossary

acquired hearing loss – hearing loss that occurs to a person born with hearing

audiogram – a graph which displays the results of a hearing test

audiologist – a specialist trained to diagnose hearing disorders

auditory processing disorder (APD) – difficulty recognizing subtle differences in sound, i.e., "pen-pin"

aural habilitation – the practice of having students with hearing loss work with their residual hearing

bilateral hearing loss – hearing loss in both ears

central auditory processing disorder (CAPD) – a condition in which auditory centers of the brain become damaged affecting a person's ability to discriminate or localize sounds

central hearing loss – hearing loss that results from damage to the nerves of the central nervous system whether in the pathways to the brain or in the brain itself

cochlear implant – a surgically implanted device that converts sound into electrical impulses stimulating the auditory nerve fibers to allow hearing

conductive hearing loss – damage in the middle ear that causes some hearing loss but can be treated medically

congenital hearing loss – hearing loss that is present at birth

deaf culture / deaf community – a unique culture of people with hearing loss who communicate through manual language

decibel – a unit of loudness

hard of hearing – having some hearing loss but able to hear with amplification

mixed hearing loss – a combination of conductive and sensorineural hearing loss

otitis media – inflammation of the middle ear (the most common form of an earache)

otologist – a doctor who specializes in problems of the ear *postlingual hearing loss* – hearing loss that occurs after the child has learned to talk

prelingual hearing loss – hearing loss that occurs before the child has learned to talk

residual hearing – hearing ability that remains when there is a hearing loss

sensorineural hearing loss – damage to the sensory nerve in the inner ear, usually resulting in irreversible and permanent hearing loss

T.D.D. – Telephone Devises for the Deaf

T.T. – Text Telephone; a device which allows typed messages to be sent over telephone lines

tinnitus – a perception of sound in the ear, usually a ringing when there is no external source

unilateral hearing loss – hearing loss in only one ear

Reference Books

Kluwin, Thomas N., Donald F. Moores and Martha G. Gaustad, eds. *Toward Effective Public School Programs for Deaf Students: Context, Process, and Outcomes.* New York, NY: Teachers College Press, 1992.

Mindel, Eugene D. and McCay Vernon, eds. *They Grow in Silence: Understanding Deaf Children and Adults.* Austin, TX: PRO-ED, Inc.,1987.

Moores, Donald F. *Educating the Deaf: Psychology, Principles, and Practices.* 5th ed. Boston, MA: Houghton Miflin, 2000.

Schirmer, Barbara R. *Language and Literacy Development in Children Who Are Deaf.* 2nd ed. Boston, MA: Allyn & Bacon, 2000.

Schwartz, Sue, ed. *Choices in Deafness: A Parent's Guide.* Bethesda, MD: Woodbine House, 1987.

Stewart, David A. and Thomas N. Kluwin. *Teaching Deaf and Hard of Hearing Students.* Needham Heights, MA: Allyn and Bacon, 2000.

Web Sites

American Speech-Language-Hearing Association (ASHA)
www.asha.org

Closed-Captioned Videos
www.cfv.org

Council on Education for the Deaf
www.educ.kent.edu/deafed

Deaf Education
www.deafed.net

Deaf Sign
www.deafsign.com

Information on Education of the Deaf
www.questia.com

National Association for the Deaf
www.nad.org

Chapter X

Students with Low Vision and Blindness

- *Students with Low Vision*
- *Students with Blindness*

Definition

Visually handicapped means a visual impairment that, even with correction, adversely affects a child's educational performance.
—IDEA

Important Facts about
Students with Low Vision and Blindness

- Normal vision is 20/20 and normal visual field is 160 degrees.

- Many people who are legally blind have some residual vision.

- People with blindness do not develop better hearing. They simply learn to use their hearing to better advantage.

- Many people with blindness do not read Braille or do not read it fluently. People with blindness are more dependent on hearing written material read to them.

- The most important things a blind person must learn are orientation, mobility and independent living.

- Blindness has no relation to intelligence. The scholastic expectations of a student with blindness should be the same as those of sighted students. However, the amount of work produced may differ.

- People with low vision who can navigate without a white cane may do so solely to prevent others from expecting them to perform tasks they may be unable to do.

- People with blindness can learn the names of things but may not learn their characteristics or specific details.

- There are a growing number of technological advances, many quite expensive, that have been made to help the blind have better orientation, mobility and instruction in school.

- Schools may be reluctant to purchase many of the devices to aid vision because of the high cost.

- Sighted students can visualize a whole learning activity and then seek to understand each part. Students with blindness must learn the parts and then develop an understanding of the whole.

- Students with blindness cannot determine cause and effect as

126

easily as sighted children because they cannot observe the result of an action.

- Students with blindness do not have equal opportunity for incidental learning because they cannot observe the activity going on around them.

- Students with blindness do not have equal opportunity to learn vocabulary because early vocabulary is built on naming familiar objects.

- Students with blindness have difficulty learning behavioral nuances necessary for successful socialization.

- Students with blindness are not able to participate in some early skill-building activities.

- Students with acquired blindness (those who were born with eyesight but have lost it) may harbor anger over their situation. They may take it out on the teacher by saying things such as "How would you like to be blind?"

- Students with blindness are accustomed to terms such as "look here" or "see what I mean" and are not offended by them.

- Parents of students with blindness sometimes have difficulty bonding with their children because a blind child does not gaze into their eyes the way sighted children do. The parents may not play as long with a blind child as with a sighted child.

- Most schools provide students with a yearly vision screening, which merely alerts parents of a vision problem that should be looked into. The students are usually given a note to bring home to their parents, which means the parents may or may not receive the note.

- Guide dogs are not pets. They are allowed in the school as well as all public places, including restaurants. They are working dogs and are not in class for the other children to play with. Permission should be sought before petting or interacting with a guide dog.

- If people wish to take a student with blindness by the arm in order to serve as a guide, they should ask permission from the blind student first. While moving with a blind student it is helpful to describe where you are going and what you are passing.

- People who are legally blind are entitled to certain benefits, such as an extra tax deduction on their income tax.

Students with Low Vision

Definition

Low vision is a condition in which a person can read only with the assistance of magnifying aids and/or large print.

Characteristics of Students with Low Vision

- Display uneven abilities in different areas.

- See and work better on some days than on others.

- Adapt well socially and educationally.

- Are capable of adhering to class standards of discipline and behavior.

- May not be able to scan reading material or locate needed information at a glance.

- May also have a learning disability misinterpreted as a vision-related problem.

Characteristics of
Students with Undiagnosed Vision Problems

- Squint, blink and constantly rub their eyes.

- Strain to see the blackboard.

- Lack coordinated eye movement.

- Are oversensitive to light.

- Have eyes that itch, burn or tear.

- Have headaches.

- Feel nauseous.

- Hold books too close or too far away from the face.

- Move books in closer and out farther from the face while reading.

- Shut or cover one eye while reading.

- Read for a brief period and then put the reading material down in order to rest.

- Tend to lose their place when reading.

- Confuse similar looking letters.

- Guess at words when reading.

- Align writing poorly.

Suggestions for Working with a Student with Low Vision

- Request a Functional Vision Assessment from the student's doctor to help determine the activities in which the student can participate.

- Seat the student near windows at the front of the room to provide natural light and avoid the glare of the sun.

- Allow the student to choose seats for different activities if it will help the student see better.

- Allow a student bothered by the glare of overhead lighting to wear a cap with a visor.

- Ask the student to assist you when doing a class demonstration, which will allow the student to stand near you and see better.

- Keep a large magnifying glass available.

- Provide a mini reading lamp.

- If the student is in the habit of forgetting his glasses at home, arrange with the parents to have an extra pair in school.

- Provide the student with pencils that have soft dark lead.

- Provide boldly lined paper for writing.

- When preparing handouts use Roman type standard, serif, or sans serif types, which are easiest to read.

- Print with black ink on a white or light yellow paper with matte finish for the best contrast.

- For greater contrast and readability use an overhead projector rather than writing on the chalkboard.

- Acquire a set of large-print textbooks, workbooks and reading materials.

- Try to acquire assistive technologies, such as screen enlargement programs, screen reader programs, speech recognition software and closed circuit television.

- Talk to the parents and the special education teacher about the availability of vision aids for the classroom. Become an advocate for the student to help obtain whatever devices are necessary.

- If it is difficult to obtain mechanical or technological devices due to high cost and shortage of school funds, consider making it a class project to raise the money.

- Use real objects to illustrate lectures.

- Provide the student with lesson plans or outlines in advance to make it easier to follow your lessons.

- Allow the student to tape-record your lessons to play back at home.

- Allow the student to complete written assignments by speaking into a tape recorder.

- When giving a written test, give it with questions and spaces for answers on the same paper.

- Allow the student extra time to do classwork.

- Allow the student to get help from other students when reading becomes tiring.

- Modify homework assignments by omitting easy work and reducing the number of problems that must be completed.

- When a student does well, give verbal affirmations, as smiles or other reactions may not be seen.

- Help the student develop social skills.

- Look for alternatives to games in which a small ball must be hit or caught.

- When going on field trips, mention that one of your students has low vision. Many museums have special programs and assistive devices to accommodate them.

Students with Blindness

Definitions

functionally blind – some residual vision, insufficient to read print and requiring other senses to perform daily living activities

legally blind (a legal term) – less than 20/200 in the better eye with correction or a field of vision which is less than 20 degrees

totally blind – no vision and total dependence on other senses to perform daily living activities

In this text the term "blindness" includes functionally blind, legally blind and totally blind.

Characteristics of Students with Blindness

- Exhibit a wide range of behavior largely determined by the time of onset of their blindness—those who developed blindness have knowledge and skills that children born blind do not have.

- May need to be introduced to people in social situations, as they may feel different than sighted people and isolate themselves.

- May have low self-esteem because they cannot do some things sighted people can do.

- May feel clumsy because they bump into things.

- May perform self-stimulating behaviors, such as hitting their head and face, scratching their eyes, rocking, etc.

- Prone to accidents and injury.

- Adjust well in most classes.

- Will have vocabulary deficits.

- May have social skill deficits.

Suggestions for Working with a Student with Blindness

- Request Braille copies of workbooks and textbooks.

- Try to acquire assistive technology, such as screen-reader programs, note-taking devices, speech recognition software and talking dictionaries.

- Encourage the student to explore the classroom and school.

- Provide the student with additional storage space, if necessary.

- Privately check, or have a friend of the student privately check, that the student is correctly dressed (buttons, zippers, snaps, etc.) when entering school.

- Though there is a tendency to be overprotective of a student with blindness, allow the student to take some risks, particularly on the playground.

- Give the student a normal amount of praise. Do not be excessive.

- If the student has an outburst of anger due to acquired blindness, do not be offended. Assure the student that you are available to help with the work for the entire school year.

- Try to eliminate the student's self-stimulating behaviors.

- Help develop orientation and mobility skills.

- Plan activities to help the student develop social skills.

- Develop daily-living skills.

- Develop organizational skills.

- Develop communication skills.

- Develop career and recreational skills.

- Help the student learn to listen critically.

- Spell unfamiliar words used in the lessons.

- Keep background noise to a minimum so the student can hear what is going on.

- Use tactile objects as much as possible.

- In geography try to provide the student with relief maps.

- In art encourage the student to work with varied materials.

- In math allow the student to do only the number of problems necessary to gain the skill.

- In math allow the student to use a talking calculator.

- In geometry, figures can be presented by stitching over the lines of a worksheet with a sewing machine.

- In PE encourage exercises and activities which promote increased strength and body coordination.

- In PE provide exercises that promote gross motor movement and spontaneous movement.

- Encourage the student to participate in music and drama.

- Allow lessons to be tape-recorded for review at home.

- Allow the student to speak into a tape recorder to complete written assignments.

- Be clear and specific when giving instructions.

- Allow the student to skip over easy parts of the assignments.

- Allow extra time to complete assignments.

- Involve the entire class. Use study-buddies to help the student with recording assignments, taking notes, moving from room to room, etc. When writing on the chalkboard have the buddy read what is being written.

- Include the student in all classroom activities.

- Assign the student appropriate chores.

- During class discussions have all the students identify themselves before speaking.

- Teach the class not to move furniture or leave belongings lying around on the floor.

- Plan group activities which involve discussion and planning.

- Expect the same standards of behavior you expect from all your other students.

- Help the student meet other people with blindness in the community, especially successful people with blindness who could be good role models.

Glossary

acquired blindness – blindness that develops or occurs after birth *albinism* – a hereditary condition characterized by lack of the pigment melanin causing a loss of visual acuity and extreme sensitivity to sunlight

amblyopia – a condition in which vision in one eye is reduced because the eye and the brain are not working together (also called *lazy eye*)

astigmatism – a condition caused by an irregularly shaped cornea causing objects to look blurred

cataracts – a clouding of the lens in the eye causing unclear vision

color blindness – the inability to see some or all colors (more common in boys than girls)

congenital blindness – blindness present since birth

conjunctivitis – inflammation of the thin membrane covering the front of the eye (also called *pink eye*)

cross-eyed – a condition in which the pupils both go to the inner part of the cornea (see *strabismus*)

diabetic retinopathy – a condition in which poor blood circulation through the vessels in the retina causes damage and possible blindness

diplopia – blurred or double vision

farsightedness – (see *hyperopia*)

glaucoma – a condition in which fluid collects inside the eye causing pressure and damage to the optic nerve

Hoover cane – the red and white cane used by the blind to aid in orientation and mobility

hyperopia – a condition that blurs sight of near objects but retains clear vision of objects that are far away (also called *farsightedness*)

lazy eye – (see *amblyopia*)

macular degeneration – a condition in which the ability to see color and detail becomes impaired

myopia – a condition that blurs the sight of far objects but retains clear vision of objects that are near (also called *nearsightedness*)

nearsightedness – (see *myopia*)

nystagmus – repetitive involuntary movement of the eye that causes lack of visual acuity

optic nerve atrophy – a disorder of the optic nerve that results in reduced visual acuity or low vision

optic nerve hypoplasia – a disorder of the optic nerve that results in a visual impairment or blindness

photophobia – sensitivity to light

pink eye – (see *conjunctivitis*)

retinitis pigmentosa – a progressive eye disease caused by a deposit of pigmentation on the back of the retina resulting in a small field of vision

retinopathy of prematurity – damage to the retina, which may lead to blindness, caused by excessive oxygen given to premature babies

scotoma – a blind spot or hole in the visual field

Snellen Chart – the chart used in a doctor's office to test visual acuity

strabismus – a problem with the eye muscles causing a person to appear cross-eyed or wall-eyed and possibly leading to reduced or lost vision in the weaker eye

tunnel vision – a condition which allows the viewer to see only a small area at a time

visual acuity – the measure of how well a person can see

visual field – the area a person can see without moving the eyes or head, normally about 160 degrees

wall-eyed – a condition in which one or both eyes involuntarily go to the outer sides of the cornea (see *strabismus*)

Reference Books

Lewis, S. and C. B. Allman. *Seeing Eye to Eye: An Administrators Guide to Students with Low Vision*. New York, NY: AFP Press, 2000.

Olmstead, Jean E. *Itinerant Teaching: Tricks of the Trade for Teachers of Blind and Visually Impaired Students*. New York, NY: American Foundation for the Blind, 1991.

Rug, Sally M. *Helping the Visually Impaired Child with Developmental Problems: Effective Practice in Home School and Community.* New York, NY: Teachers College Press, 1988.

Scholl, Geraldine T. *Foundations of Education for Blind and Visually Handicapped Children and Youth; Theory and Practice.* New York, NY: American Foundation for the Blind, 1986.

Web Sites

American Council for the Blind
www.acb.org

American Foundation for the Blind
www.afb.org/afb

American Printing House for the Blind
www.aph.org

Association for Education and Rehabilitation of the Blind and Visually Impaired
www.aerbvi.org

National Foundation of the Blind
www.nfb.org

Prevent Blindness America
www.preventblindness.org

Chapter XI

Students with Traumatic Brain Injury

Definition

Traumatic brain injury is an acquired injury to the brain caused by an external physical force, resulting in total or partial functional disability or psychosocial impairment, or both, that adversely affects a child's educational performance. The term applies to open or closed head injuries resulting in impairments in one or more areas, such as cognition; language; memory; attention; reasoning; abstract thinking; judgment; problem-solving; sensory, perceptual, and motor abilities; psychosocial behavior; physical functions; information processing; and speech. The term does not apply to brain injuries that are congenital or degenerative, or brain injuries induced by birth trauma.

—IDEA

Important Facts about
Students with Traumatic Brain Injury

• The three main causes of traumatic brain injury are automobile accidents, sports and recreational accidents, and violence.

• Males are three times more likely to receive a traumatic brain injury than females.

• The most likely age to incur traumatic brain injury is 15 to 24.

• Traumatic brain injury is the most common cause of death and injury in children and young adults.

• After an injury it is usual for a neurologist to conduct an informal, bedside evaluation in the areas of attention, memory and the ability to understand and talk.

• Traumatic brain injury can be mild, moderate or severe depending on the length of the coma and the extent of the injury.

• Students may have undiagnosed closed-head traumatic brain injury, particularly shaken-impact or shaken baby syndrome, due to child abuse.

• All cases of traumatic brain injury have their own manifestations. Every case is different.

• Thirty years ago 90 percent of people who suffered brain injuries died. Due to advances in science and medicine, the figure today is 50 percent. Consequently the classroom teacher can expect to encounter more students with traumatic brain injury.

- The most prevalent type of injuries are cognitive.

- Cognitive impairments may be the underlying cause in behavioral problems, such as anger, depression, missing classes and appointments, misunderstanding course material and assignments, inability to make decisions, difficulty in managing frustration, and social inappropriateness.

- IQ tests may not reveal a traumatic brain injury as the abilities lost are more likely new learning as opposed to past learning.

- Severe traumatic brain injury may limit educational goals to improving communication and self-help skills.

- It is important to the student's recovery that the school has a plan in place developed by both educational and medical staffs before the student returns from hospitalization or convalescence.

- Although the student may recover from traumatic brain injury, it is likely the incident will cause some permanent changes in behavior.

- Problems resulting from traumatic brain injury may not develop immediately or for several years. Small children may not exhibit problems until failing to reach certain milestones of maturity.

- The effects of traumatic brain injury change as the brain repairs itself or learns to redirect its functioning. Many are not noticeable immediately. Some may appear days or weeks later. Therefore, the student's abilities should be reassessed frequently.

- Students with traumatic brain injury may have little ability for self-motivation, which can be mistaken for laziness or nonchalance.

- In addition to coping with skills lost, the student must also cope with a slowed process of learning new skills.

- Sports injuries often go unreported. Teachers should watch for symptoms, such as headaches or sudden slurred speech.

- Students who suffer from traumatic brain injury understand their problem. They are often angry and frustrated because they can no longer perform certain tasks with the skill they once had.

- While recovering from an accident involving traumatic brain injury, the student may receive some schooling in the hospital or at home. However, the student should be encouraged to return to school as soon as possible.

Characteristics of Students with Traumatic Brain Injury

Physical behaviors

- Have lost skills in some areas but not in others. (This is particularly true in open head wounds in which only the areas of the brain touched by the wound are affected.)

- Have epileptic seizures.

- Show signs of paralysis or spasticity.

- Exhibit coordination problems.

- Forget how to do complex physical functions.

- React adversely to touch or smell.

- Exhibit weakness, fatigue or problems with sleeping.

- Have frequent headaches.

- Develop vision or hearing problems.

Cognitive behaviors

- Have difficulty concentrating or paying attention.

- Have problems with both long and short term memory.

- Have difficulty solving problems and reasoning.

- Think more slowly.

- Have difficulty planning and sequencing.

- Demonstrate poor judgment and lack of insight.

- Exhibit loss of some academic abilities.

Linguistic behaviors

- Unable to speak for a period of time (*aphasia*). (Expressive language is usually recovered as the wounds heal.)

140

- Revert to immature language.

- Have problems understanding language.

- Speak slowly.

- Have difficulty finding the right word.

- Have difficulty following directions.

Psychological behaviors

- Exhibit personality changes.

- Have difficulty with self-identity.

- Exhibit increased egocentrism.

- Respond with increased or decreased emotion.

- Are depressed, irritable or anxious.

- Exhibit poor coping abilities and reduced social skills.

- Are fearful of new situations.

- May blurt out rude and inappropriate remarks.

Suggestions for Working with a Student with Traumatic Brain Injury

- Revolve student's education around a four point program: (1) try to recover old skills, (2) compensate for unrecoverable skills, (3) develop new skills, and (4) help student and classmates adjust to any personality changes.

- Because of changes in abilities due to healing, review and revise the IEP every few weeks.

- The IEPs should be made flexible enough to allow the teacher to make necessary instructional changes without having to keep calling for new IEP meetings.

- Focus teaching on a good recovery rather than a full recovery.

- Provide feedback to the student about how and what he is doing.

- Help the rest of the class understand the nature of the student's changes in behavior and encourage them to remain friends.

- Assign a classmate to help the student understand all his assignments and, if necessary, give help throughout the day's activities.

- Allow the student to use necessary devices, such as a tape recorder or a calculator.

- Keep good records of what the student is learning and what he is not learning.

- Assess the student by comparing the level of work before the injury to the present level of work.

- Allow the student to take periods of rest as needed to relieve the fatigue often associated with recent traumatic brain injury.

- Try to reinforce the work being done by the ancillary staff (speech therapist, occupational therapist, physical therapist, social worker, tutor, etc.) who are working with the student.

- Capitalize on retained skills and abilities.

- Develop rewards programs to encourage positive changes in behavior.

- Link new material to prior knowledge.

- Give the student check lists for completing tasks.

- Define words or use synonyms if the student does not understand what is being said.

- Provide the student with both verbal and written instructions. Check for accuracy.

- Repeat verbal instructions. Use different ways of saying what you want to express if the student does not seem to understand the instructions the first time.

- If the student is having trouble concentrating, allow him to wear earphones or to sit facing the wall.

- If the student is unable to contend with lengthy instructions, shorten instruction times and give the student opportunities to rest.

- Reduce the number of times the student has to do two or more things at once, such as listening and taking notes.

- If necessary, modify classwork and homework expectations.

- Structure lessons to include several small group discussions.

- Allow the student extra time to finish work.

- Assist the student in keeping his desk, work and books neat and orderly.

- Post assignments in the same place and in the same manner each day.

- Teach the student to use a daily organizer, fact sheets and highlighters.

- Do not allow the student to guess answers. Tell the student the answer instead and work with the student to reinforce remembering it.

- Use repetition.

- Insist on appropriate work and appropriate classroom behavior.

To improve attention

- Remove distractions, such as books and supplies, not necessary for the immediate work.

- Limit the amount of information given at one time.

- Adjust the assignments to be compatible with the student's attention span.

- Bring the student into focus with statements calling attention to what you are about to do.

To improve language comprehension and the ability to follow directions

- Limit the amount of directives to one or two at a time.

- Use language that is concrete.

- Tell the student to ask for more information if he doesn't understand what to do.

- Use examples and pictures to help the student understand.

- Use gestures and body language to help clarify directions.

To improve memory

- Have a classmate help the student take notes.

- Relate new facts to known facts.

143

- Have the student keep a journal of the day's activities and assignments.

- Highlight key information in the readings.

- Provide the student with a schedule of the day's activities.

- Have the student repeat important information back to you. Allow the student to practice repeating key information.

- Have the student write key facts on his assignments, such as who, what, why, when and where.

- Have the student use adhesive note pads to remember where to locate recently covered reading material.

- Provide the student with pictures and other visual cues.

- Practice rote memorization.

- Continually ask the student to restate new information.

To improve sequencing

- Break each task into smaller steps. List and number each step. Assign the steps to the student one at a time.

- Start the student with two or three steps in the sequence. Tell the student how many steps remain. Provide models and examples.

- Give cues to the student to help him remember the next step.

- Provide written directions or diagrams that will cue the next step.

To improve organization

- Teach the student to place thoughts into categories.

- Focus on one type of information at a time.

- Encourage the student to try to organize slowly and thoroughly before beginning a lesson.

To improve generalization

- Provide the student with a format for solving math problems. Help him to use the format in more than one situation.

- Present concrete facts first and relate abstractions to them.

- Provide the student with samples of work which were done correctly.

144

- Do similar work in two different ways, such as answering questions by filling in the blanks on a worksheet and then on a computer.

Brain Area Relationships

frontal lobe (above the eyes) – seat of problem solving, judgment, inhibition of behavior, planning, motor planning, personality, emotions, organization, attention and speaking (Injury to this area can cause loss of body movement, decreased ability to interact with others, mood changes, difficulty in problem solving and change in personality.)

parietal lobe (top of the head) – seat of visual perception, spatial perception, sense of touch and ability to differentiate size, shape and color (Injury to this area can cause reading problems, speaking problems, problems with math, and loss of ability to do more than one thing at a time.)

occipital lobe (back of the head) – seat of vision (Injury to this area can cause vision problems, reading problems and writing problems.)

temporal lobe (above the ear) – seat of memory, speech, hearing, organization, and understanding language (Injury to this area can cause aggressive behavior and problems with short term memory and understanding spoken words.)

cerebellum (base of the back of the head) – seat of balance, coordination and skilled motor activity (Injury to this area can cause loss of coordination, inability to walk, tremors and slurred speech.)

brain stem (where neck meets head) – seat of breathing, heart rate, arousal, attention, sleep and concentration (Injury to this area can cause sleep problems, problems in organizing and decreased breathing capacity.)

Glossary

acquired brain injury – any injury to the brain either traumatic or non-traumatic

agnosia – inability to recognize familiar objects

amnesia – lack of memory about events over a certain period of time

anomia – inability to find the right word

145

anoxia – termination of oxygen flow to the brain causing death of brain cells (also called *hypoxia*)

aphasia – partial or total loss of speech

apraxia – inability to carry out complex or skilled movements

cognitive training – instruction to regain lost psychological processes

concussion – a condition of impaired brain functioning from an impact or blow

contusion – a bruising

dysarthria – problems with speech (slurring, slow speech, etc.) caused by a brain injury

edema – swelling

executive functions – abilities to prioritize, shift topics, think abstractly and plan ahead

Glasgow Coma Scale – a standardized system used to assess the degree of brain impairment and serious injury

hypoxia – (see *anoxia*)

lobe – a section of the brain

non-traumatic brain injury – damage to the brain caused by toxins, infections, strokes, tumors and anoxic injuries

shaken impact syndrome – brain trauma inflicted at an early age by an adult violently shaking a child so that the head moves back and forth rapidly, causing the brain to be injured from hitting the inside of the skull (also called *shaken baby syndrome*)

trauma – a physical or psychological blow

Reference Books

Appleton, R. and T. Baldwin. *Management of the Brain Injured Child.* New York, NY: Oxford University Press, 1998.

Gronwall, Dorothy, Philip Wrightson and Peter Waddel. *Head Injury: The Facts.* Oxford, UK: Oxford University Press, 1998.

Stein, Donald G., Simon Brailowsky and Bruno Will. *Brain Repair*. Oxford, UK: Oxford University Press, 1997.

Stoler, Diane Roberts, and Barbara Albers Hill. *Coping with Mild TBI*. New York, NY: Avery Hill Publishing Company, 1998.

Wolcott, Gary F. and Ronald C. Savage, eds. *An Educator's Manual: What Educators Need to Know About Students With Brain Injury*. Wamego, KS: National Head Injury Foundation, 1995.

Web Sites

Brain Injury Association
www.biausa.org

Head Injury Hotline
www.headinjury.com

National Resource Center for Traumatic Brain Injury
www.neuro.pmr.vcu.edu

The Perspectives Network
www.tbi.org

Traumatic Brain Injury National Data Center
www.tbindc.org

Traumatic Injury Survival Guide
www.tbiguide.com

Chapter XII

Students with Severe and Multiple Disabilities

- *Students with Severe and Multiple Disabilities*
- *Students with Severe and Profound Mental Retardation*
- *Students with Schizophrenia*

Definition

The term "children with severe disabilities" refers to children with disabilities who, because of the intensity of their physical, mental, or emotional problems, need highly specialized educational, social, psychological, and medical services in order to maximize their full potential for useful and meaningful participation in society and for self-fulfillment. The term includes those children with disabilities with severe emotional disturbance (including schizophrenia), autism, severe and profound mental retardation, and those who have two or more serious disabilities such as deaf-blindness, mental retardation and blindness, and cerebral palsy and deafness. Children with severe disabilities may experience severe speech, language, and/or perceptual-cognitive deprivations and evidence abnormal behaviors such as failure to respond to pronounced social stimuli, self-mutilation, self-stimulation, manifestation of intense and prolonged temper tantrums, and the absence of rudimentary forms of verbal control; and may also have intensely fragile physiological conditions.

—IDEA

Multiple disabilities means concomitant impairments (such as mental retardation blindness, mental retardation-orthopedic impairment, etc.) the combination of which causes such severe educational problems that they cannot be accommodated in special education programs solely for one of the impairments. The term does not include deaf-blindness.

—IDEA

Important Facts about
Students with Severe and Multiple Disabilities

- Many educators question the practice of including students with severe and multiple disabilities, severe and profound mental retardation and schizophrenia in their regular classrooms because the student is not capable of doing the classwork the rest of the class is doing. While this is true, the inability to do grade appropriate work should not exclude the student from the regular class. Students don't have to be in the class for the same reason or achieve the same level of work (which they don't anyhow). Rather, the teacher should see what work the student can

150

accomplish, how the student can participate with the class, and what gains can be made.

- The value of having students with severe and multiple disabilities, severe and profound mental retardation, and schizophrenia in a regular classroom is to give them the opportunity to interact with their non-disabled peers and to give their non-disabled peers the opportunity to interact with them.

- Students with severe disabilities, especially where intelligence is intact, may experience emotional problems, particularly depression. Family members are also subject to depression, which makes it more difficult for the student. Inclusion programs have the ability to alleviate this.

- Severe disabilities are better defined by the amount of supports the student needs than by the impairment he has.

- Disorders such as cerebral palsy, phenylketonuria (PKU), encephalocele, amniotic band syndrome and severe accidents are common causes of multiple disabilities.

- Most students with multiple disabilities have impairments in intellectual functioning and communication, as well as hearing and vision. There may also be problems in adaptive skills and motor development.

- Students with severe disabilities often have health care needs that must be attended to while in school.

- Many students have epileptic seizures as a part of their disability (see p. 181, "Suggestions for Working with a Student with Epilepsy").

- Many students with severe disabilities are dependent on various forms of assistive technology, which aid in mobility, communication and control of the environment. The teacher and the aid must learn how to use these devices. When appropriate, other students in the class should also learn.

- The curriculum for students with severe disabilities should be geared to helping the student with self-help skills, mobility, communication and ability to live in the community.

- Students with severe and multiple disabilities respond positively to warmth and human companionship. They are also capable of giving these.

- If the regular classroom teacher is having personal difficulty accepting a student with severe disabilities into the classroom, it is important to discuss this with the principal because the other students will be taking their cues of acceptance or non-acceptance of this student from the teacher.

- During the school day many students with severe and multiple disabilities need health care related to breathing, digestion and elimination. This should be the job of the aid or the school nurse. The classroom teacher should not be expected to fill this role. However, the classroom teacher may volunteer to do so if comfortable with it.

Suggestions for Working with a
Student with Severe and Multiple Disabilities

- If a student with severe disabilities is being placed in your classroom, attend the staffing and play an active role in forming the Individual Education Plan (IEP). If anything is presented that you feel is beyond your capabilities or inappropriate for a classroom teacher, attempt to work out an alternative plan.

- The following questions should be raised by the receiving classroom teacher when students with severe disabilities are being staffed:

  1. Why is this student being placed in my classroom? Is it to be with an appropriate age group or merely to satisfy the needs of the parents?
  2. What strengths does this student have? What capabilities?
  3. What are the goals for this student? Are they realistic and consistent with the abilities of the student or are they the outcome of denial and wishful thinking?
  4. What support services are being provided? Are they adequate for this student's needs?
  5. Will the student have a full-time aid? What happens on the days the aid is absent? Will the student be kept home or will the teacher have to perform the aid's duties? If a substitute aid is sent, will it be someone who is trained?
  6. What specialized services will the classroom teacher have to perform? Are these duties reasonable to require? What if the teacher feels either inadequate or uncomfortable with these duties, such as medical procedures or toileting?
  7. How will the student be graded?

- If you are required to accept a student with inadequate and inappropriate support and compromise is not possible, accept the student initially and notify the union as soon as possible. If the union cannot intervene or there is no union, do the best job possible under the circumstances. Do not take out personal frustration on the student or pass bad feelings onto other students in the class. Do not feel guilty or personally responsible for any shortfalls in the student's education. Instead, feel a sense of accomplishment for any gains made.

- There are three approaches the teacher can take in working with students with severe disabilities:

  1. the developmental approach, which tries to remediate deficits and develop skills sequentially;

  2. the functional approach, which focuses on the need to learn age-appropriate functional skills or specific tasks;

  3. the ecological approach, (the most preferred of the three) which focuses on the student and his environment and evolves as needs, goals and opportunities change.

- Recommend that the parent(s) periodically observe their child's educational process in the classroom so they can continue the process at home.

- Introduce the student to your class as you would any other new student. Encourage the classmates to introduce themselves. Introduce the aid as well

- Enact a plan with the aid to make her presence beneficial to the entire class.

- Find out what medications the student takes and what effects and reactions these medications may have. Get a written statement from the parents listing the medications, the dosages, when they are to be taken, and who is responsible for administering them.

- After the class has met the student and at a time when the student is not present, discuss the student and the nature of the student's problems with the class. Answer questions as honestly and fully as is appropriate. Encourage the parents of the student to participate in the discussion.

- Interact with the student more than merely giving the student assignments to do with the aid.

- If possible, see if any ancillary services can be performed in the classroom instead of having the student removed.

- Determine and develop the student's strengths.

- Emphasize communication skills. If possible, arrange for speech therapy.

- Students who cannot talk often communicate with gestures. Create a dictionary of gestures, adding gestures and their meanings as they develop.

- If the student cannot write his or her name, have a rubber stamp made with the student's name so the student can personalize papers.

- If the student uses a communication board, teach the student to use it effectively and allow the other students to use it to communicate with the student.

- If the student is in a wheelchair or other supportive device, make sure the student gets out of the device several times a day to exercise and sits in the device with the correct posture. If a seat belt is necessary, make sure it is secured.

- Learn what is the most comfortable working position for the student and how long that position can be maintained.

- Speak to the PE teacher about exercises the student can do in the classroom to improve movement, coordination and muscle tone.

- Allow a wheelchair-bound student free access to all parts of the room.

- Inform the class of any medical problems, such as seizures, enuresis, tics, etc. that the student is likely to display in class.

- Learn the student's special dietary needs and inform the class if certain foods are forbidden.

- Post a sign-up sheet for classmates to volunteer as helpers. Do not force students to volunteer.

- Encourage the parents of the classmates to invite the student with disabilities to birthday parties and other children's outings.

- If necessary, assure the other students that they will not "catch" the condition of the student.

- Teach self-help skills.

- Include the student in as many classroom activities as possible.

- Do not assume the student needs help. Ask the student, parents and concerned health professionals to explain specific areas in which help is needed.

- Encourage the student to feed himself, even if it is messy and takes a long time.

- Encourage the class to interact with the student on a daily basis. Each day assign one class member to be the person who may help push the wheelchair and do other necessary useful chores.

Students with Severe and Profound Mental Retardation

Definitions

Severe retardation – a condition in which a person has an IQ from 20 to 35 and requires extensive support and supervision

Profound retardation – a condition in which a person has an IQ less than 20 and requires constant support and supervision

The IQ ranges included in this section are meant to serve only as a reference and not as a solitary factor in determining the subcategories. There are other rating scales which evaluate the abilities of these students.

Important Facts about
Students with Severe and Profound Mental Retardation

- Students with severe and profound mental retardation have the following traits: *(a)* limited speech, *(b)* difficulty with mobility, *(c)* tendency to forget skills through disuse, *(d)* trouble generalizing skills, and *(e)* need for support in major life activities.

- Severe and profound mental retardation may be associated with another disability, such as cerebral palsy.

- Students with severe and profound mental retardation respond positively to contact and acceptance from adults and peers.

155

Suggestions for Working with a
Student with Severe and Profound Mental Retardation

• Welcome the student and the accompanying aid to the class and introduce them to the other students. Continue to treat the student like any other new student.

• Interact with the student beyond giving assignments to the aid. With the aid, determine your role and the role of the aid.

• Allow the student's aid to work with other students in the class.

• Allow the student's classmates to ask questions about the student and the aid. Answer the questions as honestly and as fully as is age-appropriate. Invite the student's parents to participate in the discussion.

• Encourage the class to work with the student by reading, talking, drawing or eating with the student, pushing the student's wheelchair, or doing anything appropriate that would enrich both the disabled and the regular students.

• Provide the student with a functional curriculum, which stresses communication and self-care and encourages the participation of classmates.

• If the student shows preference in learning through one particular sense (i.e. vision, hearing, touch, etc), emphasize teaching through that sense.

• If the student is capable, give instruction about health, safety and the community.

• Provide opportunities for the student to learn socialization and home-living skills.

• Provide exercises that enforce better understanding, cause and effect, naming and functioning.

• Include the student in as many classroom activities as possible.

• If possible, have the student take part in making plans for his curriculum.

• If the student receives additional services outside the classroom, try to schedule these services so the student receives maximum participation in the classroom.

Students with Schizophrenia

Definition

[Schizophrenia exhibits these] characteristic symptoms: Two (or more) of the following, each present for a significant portion of time during a 1-month period (or less if successfully treated): (1) delusions (2) hallucinations (3) disorganized speech (e.g. frequent derailment or incoherence) (4) grossly disorganized catatonic behavior (5) negative symptoms i.e. affective flattening, alogia or avolition...

—American Psychiatric Association

(Reprinted with permission from the *Diagnostic and Statistical Manual of Mental Disorders*, Fourth Edition. Copyright 1994 American Psychiatric Association.)

Important Facts about Students with Schizophrenia

- Contrary to popular opinion, the term "schizophrenia" does not mean split personality nor does it refer to people with more than one personality (multiple personality disorder), such as portrayed in the movies "Sybil" and "Three Faces of Eve." The term "schizophrenia" really means shattered personality.

- Schizophrenia has varying degrees of severity. Some students exhibit constant symptoms, while others have episodes that come and go.

- Some students with schizophrenia can control the effects with medication. Though the medication often produces side effects, such as drowsiness, tremors and decreased attention, these side effects are preferable to the student having schizophrenic symptoms.

- Medications for schizophrenia have become dramatically more effective within the last decade.

- The incidence of schizophrenia is low among younger children but increases in junior and senior high school, as puberty is the common time of onset.

- In some cases students with schizophrenia can cause harm to themselves or others. The classroom teacher needs to know if this is the case.

- It is beneficial to have an aid for a student with schizophrenia.

- Students who take medication for controlling symptoms of schizophrenia commonly experiment with skipping their medication. The teacher needs to know if the student has done this because the results can be disastrous.

- Some students with schizophrenia learn to function in society by the time they reach adulthood. Others do not.

Characteristics of Students with Schizophrenia

- Neglect personal care.

- Lack friends.

- Withdraw to a point of not responding to anyone.

- Are depressed.

- Have extreme and sudden mood changes.

- Do schoolwork poorly.

- Exhibit emotions inappropriate to the situation.

- Act in a bizarre manner.

- Tell of personal experiences the listener finds difficult to believe.

- Talk in an unusual and incomprehensible manner, often using unknown words.

- Interpret the environment and past events in an unusual manner.

- Exhibit obsessive behavior more severe than a student with obsessive/compulsive disorder.

- Have a vivid imagination (related to hallucinations and delusions).

- Talk to themselves.

- Are afraid for irrational reasons or reasons they cannot explain.

Suggestions for Working with a Student with Schizophrenia

- Focus on teaching in areas in which the student needs learning.

- Allow for flexibility in complying with classroom activities.

- Establish a plan to accommodate the student if the student's behavior prevents participation in classroom activities.

- When the student is acting appropriately, include the student in as many classroom activities as possible.

- Inquire about the student's medication and its side effects. Be prepared to accommodate the side effects when they occur.

- If the student is taking medication, make sure the medication has been taken.

- If an aid is already present in the room for another student, discuss with the administration whether the aid can play a role in the education of the student with schizophrenia.

- If the student's condition could possible threaten classroom safety, devise a plan to protect the student, classmates, the aid and yourself if a dangerous situation should arise. If the student's condition continually threatens classroom safety, question the advisability of the inclusion placement.

Glossary

affective flattening – restriction in the range of emotional expression

alogia – inability to speak because of a mental difficulty or an episode of dementia

augmentive communication – communication other than reading, writing or speaking

avolition – inability to initiate goal-directed behavior

catatonic – a type of behavior characterized by mental stupor and a rigid body that appears to be frozen in position, alternating with periods of extreme excitement

childhood psychosis – (see *pervasive development disorder*)

clean intermittent catheterization (CIC) – the insertion of a catheter into the urethra to drain urine

community-based instruction – teaching life skills in the actual setting in which the skills will be used

delusion – a mistake in thinking that results in an incorrect interpretation of events taking place

echolalia – the parroting of words or phrases usually, but not necessarily, immediately after they are heard

ecological assessment – an examination of the environments in which the student will be functioning and identification of the specific skills the student will need in order to function in them

encephalocele – a disorder in which the skull does not close but develops a membrane to cover the brain tissue

encopresis/enuresis – incontinence of feces and urine (often a symptom of a severe disability

functional curriculum – a curriculum which focuses on developing skills in communication, self-care, home living, community living, socialization and job skills

gastrostomy – tube feeding; feeding directly into the intestine through a tube

hallucination – a sensory misinterpretation of an experience

mania – excessive excitement usually centered on a specific object or event

MAPS (Making Action Plans) – a process for personalizing a particular student's education by considering his specific strengths and needs

neologism – a word coined by a person with schizophrenia which has no meaning to other people

neuroleptics – anti-psychotic drugs that suppress the symptoms of schizophrenia

pervasive developmental disorder – a distortion or lag in all or several areas of personal development

psychotic disorder – an emotional disorder or behavioral disorder characterized by bizarre thinking, feeling and acting

respiratory ventilation – a procedure for suctioning off mucus through a small tube

stereotypical behavior – persistent repetition of an action or speech pattern

The Tech Act (Technology Related Assistance to Individuals with Disabilities Act of 1988) – a federal act that authorizes funds for state systems to deliver technology and technological services to people with disabilities

Reference Books

Batshaw, Mark L., ed. *Children with Disabilities.* 5th ed. Baltimore, MD: Brookes Publishing Company, 2002.

Downing, June, Joanne Eichinger and Maryann Demchak. *Including Students With Severe and Multiple Disabilities in Typical Classrooms: Practical Strategies for Teachers.* 2nd ed. Baltimore, MD: Brookes Publishing Company, 2001.

Ferguson, Dianne. *The Challenge of Integrating Students with Severe Disabilities.* Syracuse, NY: Syracuse University, 1981.

Orelove, Fred P. and Dick Sobsey. *Educating Children With Multiple Disabilities: A Transdisciplinary Approach.* 3rd ed. Baltimore, MD: Brookes Publishing Company, 1996.

Thompson, Barbara. *A Circle of Inclusion: Facilitating the Inclusion of Young Children with Severe Disabilities in Mainstream Early Childhood Education Programs.* Lawrence, KS: University of Kansas Press, 1993.

Web Sites

The Arc
www.thearc.org

Association for Persons with Severe Handicaps
www.TASH.org

Facts for Families
www.aacap.org/factsfam

Mental Retardation Research Center
www.mrrc.npi.ucla.edu

National Alliance for Research on Schizophrenia and Depression
www.narsad.org

National Mental Health Information Center
www.mentalhealth.com

Chapter XIII

Students with Physical Disabilities

- *Students with Neurological Conditions*
  - —*Students with Cerebral Palsy*
  - —*Students with Spina Bifida*

- *Students with Musculoskeletal Conditions*
  - —*Students with Juvenile Rheumatoid Arthritis*
  - —*Students with Muscular Dystrophy*

- *Students with Spinal Cord Injuries*

Definition

"Physical disability" or "orthopedic impairment" means a severe orthopedic impairment that adversely affects a child's educational performance. The term includes impairment caused by a congenital anomaly (club foot, missing limb), impairments caused by disease (polio), and impairments from other causes, (cerebral palsy, amputation, fracture, burns that cause contractures).

—IDEA

(Traumatic brain injury is covered in Chapter XI – Students with Traumatic Brain Injury.)

Important Facts about Students with Physical Disabilities

• A physical disability is a condition that incapacitates to some degree the skeletal and/or neuromuscular systems of the body.

• A physical disability may not affect the intellectual power of the student. If only bodily function is impaired, the problems can be compensated.

• A student with a physical disability should be treated as an integral part of the class, not just a person sharing the room. The teacher must model this behavior so the class can understand this.

• Students with physical disabilities are subject to teasing and physical abuse from their classmates.

• If the student has an aid: *(a)* the teacher, not the aid, is in charge of the student's education; *(b)* the teacher and the aid should determine together the aid's role with the other students; *(c)* the teacher and the aid should be as creative and flexible as they like as long as the assigned student's needs are being met.

Suggestions for Working with a
Student with Physical Disabilities

• If a student with a physical disability is becoming one of your students, talk to the class about the new student. The school nurse, the student's parents and the student may wish to join the discussion. Encourage the class to ask questions. Answer them honestly and in understandable terms.

- Before the student enters the class, inform the class that the student with a physical disability is a fellow student for whom everyone is responsible. If appropriate, assign classroom care tasks to different members of the class, such as pushing the wheelchair or helping with books or a coat. Alternate helpers so that every member of the class has an opportunity to participate. Do not force students to participate.

- Ensure that all areas of your classroom are accessible to the student so that no educational opportunities are missed.

- Do not be overly-protective. Allow a student with physical disabilities, as any other student, to explore, make mistakes and learn to start all over again.

- Although the tendency is to place a student with a wheelchair near the back door for easy access, allow the student to place her wheelchair where it suits her best and provides access to the entire room.

- Be aware that a student's prosthetic or orthopedic equipment must be in working order. Contact the parents if it is not.

- Keep classmates with colds or other health problems at a distance from students with fragile health.

- Ask the parents and school nurse to familiarize you with the student's signs of distress.

Students with Neurological Conditions

Students with Cerebral Palsy

Definition

Cerebral palsy is an impairment of the communication process between the brain and the muscles caused by damage to the brain before or during birth or during infancy and resulting in four types of abnormal physical movement:

1. *spasticity* – mild to severe exaggeration of contractions of the muscles when they are stretching;
2. *dyskenesia* – abrupt, involuntary, extraneous motor activity,

especially when under stress (also called athetoid);

3. *ataxia* – a lurching walking gait; or

4. *mixed types* – a combination of the above.

Important Facts about Students with Cerebral Palsy

- Some students will need only slight modifications to classroom procedures, while others will need major adjustments.

- Many students will need additional services such as speech therapy, occupational therapy, physical therapy or adaptive PE.

- All students with cerebral palsy will display some loss of muscle coordination.

- As many as 75 percent of children with cerebral palsy have a concomitant disability, such as epileptic seizures, incontinence, delayed development, or hearing and vision impairments.

- About 50 percent to 70 percent of students with cerebral palsy have some mental retardation.

- About 15 percent of students with cerebral palsy will also have a learning disability.

- Many students with cerebral palsy are at risk for choking. It should be established if your student has a problem with this.

Students with Spina Bifida

Definition

Spina bifida is a congenital defect in which the spine has not closed correctly causing the the spinal cord to protrude from the weak point. There are three types:

1. *spina bifida occulta* – the spinal cord and covering do not protrude and only a small portion of the spine is missing (the most mild and common type);

2. *meningocele* – the covering, but not the spinal cord, protrudes through an opening in the spine; and

3. *mylomeningocele* – the protrusion contains both the spinal cord covering and the cord or nerve roots (the most serious type).

Important Facts about Students with Spina Bifida

- The higher on the spinal cord the problem occurs, the greater the amount of the body that will be affected.

- Other problems associated with spina bifida of which the teacher and aid should be aware are *(a)* increased body temperature, *(b)* flushed skin, *(c)* excessive perspiring, *(d)* incontinence, and *(e)* propensity to sustain injuries to the legs, often without the student's awareness.

- About 25 percent of students with spina bifida will have mental retardation.

- Some children with spina bifida have hydrocephalia (the buildup of spinal fluid in the brain) and may have to wear a shunt. If the student complains of headache, has a seizure, becomes sleepy or vomits, it may be indicative of shunt failure. Medical personnel should be notified immediately.

Suggestions for Working with a Student with Cerebral Palsy or Spina Bifida

- If the student's mental capacity has been affected, strive to enhance communication, functional mobility, daily living skills and self-determination in quality of life.

- If the student's mental capacity has not been affected, provide the student with appropriate work.

- Ask the student if he wants help. Do not assume that help is needed.

- Assign the student to a group to work on a project, if possible without the help of the aid. Monitor the student's progress.

- Give the student access to all parts of the room, regardless of the student's mobility.

- Students in wheelchairs need to be monitored to ensure they are sitting with good posture and are not listing to one side or the other.

- If the student is unable to raise her hand to ask for permission or to answer questions, devise another method to communicate these needs.

- Give the student ample opportunities to exercise. Students in

167

wheelchairs need to get out of the wheelchairs periodically to do some kind of movement. Some students will need help with this.

- Classmates will be naturally curious about assistive equipment. Although they should be taught not to play with it, let them try it in a controlled setting with the student's permission.

- Involve the student in all class activities, including field trips.

- Ensure that the student is a part of the social fabric of the class.

- Talk to the parents and special education teacher about obtaining special equipment, such as pencil holders, adaptive typewriters, small weights for strengthening muscles, communication aids, book holders and adjustable tables with lip rims.

Students with Musculoskeletal Conditions

Students with Juvenile Rheumatoid Arthritis

Definition

Juvenile rheumatoid arthritis is a condition affecting the tissue lining of the joints causing them to become stiff and painful.

Important Facts about
Students with Juvenile Rheumatoid Arthritis

- Juvenile rheumatoid arthritis can also affect the heart, liver and spleen.

- Juvenile rheumatoid arthritis can be temporary of permanent.

- The condition is commonly treated with special exercise, heat treatment and aspirin to ease the pain. In addition, some children wear casts, splints or braces.

- A student with juvenile rheumatoid arthritis must use common sense to determine in which classroom and PE activities he can participate.

- Because it seems so difficult for a student with juvenile rheumatoid arthritis to do things on his own, there is a danger of helping the student too much. It is important to let such students take care of themselves as much as possible, so they have the opportunity to grow and mature as other students do.

Suggestions for Working with a
Student with Juvenile Rheumatoid Arthritis

- Provide the student with adaptive materials for writing, such as a pen holder.

- Allow the student to move around periodically to prevent stiffness.

- Accommodate the student's requirement for frequent exercise.

- Encourage the best posture possible.

- Avoid prolonged physical activity, especially writing.

- Allow the student additional time to move from room to room.

- Allow the student additional time to finish written assignments.

- If a student is having difficulty writing, assign a buddy to write for him or to take an extra set of notes using carbon paper.

- Be aware that the student may have some eye problems related to the arthritis.

- Be aware that the student may be in pain and can become touchy as a result.

- Be aware that some students will have pain from moving around and should be required to move only when necessary.

Students with Muscular Dystrophy

Definition

Muscular dystrophy is a group of progressive diseases causing weakness of the voluntary muscles. The two most common types are:

1. *Duchenne* – an inherited form characterized by muscle weakness in most of the body with death usually occurring before age 30, and

2. *Becker* – also inherited, characterized by weakness in the legs and pelvis.

Important Facts about Students with Muscular Dystrophy

- During the early phases of the disease, muscular dystrophy may affect balance, causing the student to fall over and have difficulty running and climbing stairs.

169

- Treatment is focused on controlling the symptoms and increasing the quality of life. Activity is stressed.

- The ability to walk will eventually be lost.

- The student will become prone to diseases and common infections, which are usually fatal.

- School is often disrupted by hospital stays and days spent at home.

Suggestions for Working with a
Student with Muscular Dystrophy

- Remain flexible, working around student's absences.

- Emphasize the quality of life over the completion of schoolwork.

- Model a good relationship with the student and encourage the class to maintain friendships with the student.

- Realize the student is likely to be depressed, but encourage the student to participate in classroom activities.

Students with Spinal Cord Injuries

Definition

Spinal cord injuries are accidental injuries to the spinal cord which are often the result of an automobile accident, sports accident or gunshot wound.

Important Facts about
Students with Spinal Cord Injuries

- The extent of the student's disability is determined by the amount of damage and the location of the injury. The higher on the spinal cord the injury occurs, the greater the amount of the body that will be affected.

- The student is likely to experience problems, such as breathing difficulty, lack of bladder control, skin irritations and sexual dysfunction.

- The student is likely to experience emotional problems associated with losing his old lifestyle and having to adapt to a more limited one.

Suggestions for Working with a Student with Spinal Cord Injuries

- Ensure that the student's IEP has short term goals of helping the student adjust to new conditions.

- Attempt to keep the student's life as normal as possible.

- Encourage the student's classmates to continue friendships, even if they become difficult to maintain.

- Allow the student to be depressed but encourage the student to adjust to his new situation.

- Help the student to feel connected with others.

Glossary

atonia – lack of muscle tone

atrophy – a wasting away in size of a cell, tissue, organ or part of the body caused by lack of movement, lack of activity or loss of nerve supply

colostomy – a surgical opening into the abdomen to remove the bowels

congenital – present at birth

dysarthria – inability to speak clearly

hypertonia – tightness in a muscle or muscle group

hypotonia – abnormally low tension in a muscle or muscle group

incontinence – the inability to control the bowels

jejunum tube – a tube inserted in the small intestine to provide feeding

monoplegia – paralysis of one limb

muscle tone – the resistance of a muscle to being stretched

orthosis – a brace used to support or align a physical deformity

paralysis – the loss of power and feeling to a part of the body

paraplegia – the impairment and limited use of the limbs

perinatal – the time from the twentieth week of pregnancy to the twenty-eighth day after birth

postnatal – the time from the twenty-eighth day of life onward

prenatal – the time from conception to birth

prosthesis – an artificial limb

quadriplegia – a weakness in both arms and legs

scoliosis – curvature of the spine

shunt – a tube implanted in the body to draw off excessive fluids

tracheostomy – a surgical opening in the wind pipe (trachea) into which a tube is inserted to assist breathing

Reference Books

Dormans, Paul and Louis Pellegrino. *Caring for Children with Cerebral Palsy: A Team Approach.* Baltimore, MD: Brookes Publishing Company, 1997.

Miller, Freeman. *Physically Handicapped Children.* Victoria, BC: Heritage House, 2000.

Pearson, Douglas T. *The Medically Complex Child.* Bethesda, MD: Woodbine House, 1997.

Ratto, Linda Lee. *Coping with Being Physically Challenged.* New York, NY: Rosen Publishing Group, 1991.

Sandler, Adrian. *Living with Spina Bifida: A Guide for Families and Professionals.* Chapel Hill, NC: University of North Carolina Press, 1997.

Web Sites

Cerebral Palsy Information
  www.cerebral-palsy-web.org

The Muscular Dystrophy Association
  www.mdausa.org

The National Spinal Cord Injury Association
  www.spinalcord.org

Spina Bifida Association
  www.sbaa.org

United Cerebral Palsy
  www.ucp.org

Chapter XIV

Students
with
Other Health
Impairments

- *Students with Asthma*
- *Students with Allergies*
- *Students with Juvenile Diabetes*
- *Students with Epilepsy*
- *Students with Cystic Fibrosis*
- *Students with Cancer or Leukemia*
- *Students with HIV or AIDS*
- *Students with Sickle Cell Anemia*
- *Students with Birth Defects*
- *Students with Hemophilia*
- *Students Who Hyperventilate*
- *Students Who Have Been Abused*
- *Students with Childhood Obesity*
- *Students with Other Health and Medical Impairments*

Definition

Students having Other Health Impairments are those having limited strength, vitality or alertness , including a heightened alertness to environmental stimuli, that results in limited alertness with respect to the educational environment that

1. *is due to chronic or acute health problems such as asthma, attention deficit disorder or attention deficit hyperactive disorder, diabetes, epilepsy, a heart condition, hemophilia, lead poisoning, nephritis, rheumatic fever, and sickle cell anemia; and*

2. *adversely affects a child's educational performance.*

—IDEA

Important Facts about Students with Health Impairments

• The mental ability of most students is not directly affected by their health impairments.

• The student's ability to produce, however, may be limited by the resulting frequent absences and lack of energy, strength, vitality and alertness.

• Teachers should expect periodic absences to accommodate doctor visits, medical treatments and relapses. The family, student and teacher should work out a plan to keep the student as up-to-date as possible.

• Students may suffer side effects, such as nausea or drowsiness, due to medication or medical treatments.

Suggestions for Working with a Student with Health Impairments

• The teacher should, as much as possible, keep the student up-to-date with the rest of the class.

• When the student is assigned to your classroom, arrange a meeting with the student, the parents, the school nurse and the aid, if one is provided, to discuss:

1. medical procedures that must take place in school and who is responsible for performing them (Accept responsibility for

174

only those procedures you are comfortable performing. Do not accept responsibility for a procedure you feel you cannot perform and then hope it won't be necessary.);

2. procedures in the event of a medical emergency, which should be written, formally or informally, and include symptoms to watch for, people to notify and step-by-step actions for all possible conditions (i.e., when medication is not effective);

3. what information should be shared with the class and who should be responsible for sharing it; and

4. when the plan should be revised.

- Do not hesitate to involve trustworthy classmates in your emergency plans, especially to immediately notify you if the student appears to be having difficulties.

- Provide the student with a choice of locations to take medication or give themselves injections or blood tests. The bathroom is not a good option, because it isn't clean enough for medical procedures.

- Allow the student free access to drinking water.

- Allow the student free access to the bathrooms and the nurse's office. Insist the student notify you if he is leaving the room for a medical reason, and, if possible, have him accompanied by the aid or a dependable student.

- Be aware of the general health of the student and any sign of problems, as some parents may be neglectful of their children. Make sure the school has procedures for notifying the student's family. Assure the student that she should tell you when she is not feeling well.

- Because students with health impairments may be subject to ostracism, especially if the impairment has caused physical disfigurement, the student may require emotional support from the teacher. If you have a problem providing this support, discuss the situation with the school administration.

Students with Asthma

Definition

Asthma is a chronic obstructive lung condition, which can vary in intensity from mild to life threatening.

Important Facts about Students with Asthma

- Asthma can be triggered by allergens in the air, such as pollen, dust, mold, animal hair, smoke, chalk dust and chemicals.

- Asthma can be triggered by laughing or crying too hard, upper respiratory infections and vigorous exercise.

- Asthma can be triggered by cold weather and breathing cold air.

- Moderate exercise will not trigger asthma. Strong emotions will not trigger asthma.

- Stress will not cause an asthma attack, but asthma will cause stress.

- In the past 15 years the incidence of asthma has nearly doubled and is the leading medical cause for school absence.

- On the average there will be two students with asthma in every classroom.

- Exercises, which help prevent the air passages from constricting, may alleviate an asthma attack. They are, however, only meant to give partial relief until medication can be taken.

- The most common treatment for asthma is medication taken through an inhaler. The teacher may be asked to keep the student's inhaler or an extra inhaler.

Characteristics of Students with Asthma

- Exhibit chronic breathing difficulties, such as sneezing, rasping, coughing and gasping for breath.

- May exhibit severe symptoms, such as wheezing, difficulty breathing, shortness of breath, tightness of pain in the chest, coughing throughout the day, and little energy for active play.

- Often exhibit fatigue due to lack of sleep from breathing difficulties.

- Periodically absent from school when breathing becomes too difficult.

- May exhibit side effects from medication, such as dizziness, drowsiness, over-stimulation and nausea.

176

Suggestions for Working with a Student with Asthma

- Do not allow the student to become a victim of his asthma.

- Do not allow the student to use the threat of an asthma attack to control the teacher or classroom activities.

- Ask the parents to inform you of any necessary restrictions on the student's activities. In PE do not exclude the student entirely, rather find some means of participation.

- If you are asked to decide when the student is to be given the inhaler, request a written set of guidelines from the parents.

- If you are asked to monitor the student's breathing with a peak-flow meter, request detailed information from the parents.

- Make sure the student is sitting in an upright position when taking medication through an inhaler.

- After the student takes medication, make sure the student can speak a full sentence without pausing, showing that the medication has worked. If the student is unable to do so, follow the procedures in your emergency plan.

- If you have a chalkboard in the classroom, sit the student away from it so he won't breathe the chalk dust.

- See if you can get air cleaners for your room.

Students with Allergies

Definition

Allergies are hypersensitive responses of the body to foreign substances known as allergens. (Only responses that present a problem learning in school will be considered here.)

Important Facts about Students with Allergies

- Most allergic reactions are triggered by food, medications or breathing pollen or dust. Some are triggered merely by physical contact.

- Some common substances present in the school that may cause allergic reactions are pollen, dust, latex, peanuts, milk, eggs and wheat products.

177

- Some students have violent allergic reactions and need to be treated with an "epipen" (epinephrine). If the student cannot administer this himself, he may need help from an adult in the classroom.

Characteristics of Students with Allergies

- May exhibit benign reactions, such as sneezing or itching.

- May exhibit more serious reactions, such as swelling, vomiting, cramps, diarrhea, hives, difficulty breathing or loss of consciousness.

- May experience pain with reactions such as swelling and cramps.

Suggestions for Working with a Student with Allergies

- Ask all parents to inform you of any allergies their children may have that are likely to cause a problem in the classroom. Keep a list of the children who have allergies and the substances which cause them, so the substances can be avoided in the classroom.

- If a student has violent allergic reactions that must be treated immediately, make sure the procedure to treat the reaction is included in the written plan.

- Manage such events as birthday parties to ensure that parents who wish to bring food for the entire class are meeting the needs of those students who have food aversions. This is preferable to having no such events.

Students with Juvenile Diabetes

Definition

Juvenile Diabetes is a disorder of metabolism caused by insufficient amounts of insulin produced by the body. The condition is lifelong and can be controlled through proper diet, exercise and insulin shots. There are two types of diabetes:

1. *Type 1 diabetes* – most often has its onset in childhood and must be treated by insulin injections or a pump (patches, sprays and oral insulin are being tested). About 10 percent of diabetics have type 1.

2. *Type 2 diabetes* – used to be seen only in adults but is now developing in children. Onset is gradual. Many cases of type 2

diabetes can be treated with exercise, diet and weight loss, although many people with type 2 also need to take insulin. About 90 percent of diabetics have type 2.

If treated improperly one of two conditions may occur:

1. *hyperglycemia* (also known as *diabetic coma*) – a very serious condition resulting from insufficient insulin in the body, which can cause the student to lapse into a coma. Symptoms may include fatigue, thirst, trouble breathing, hot and dry skin, or blurred vision. Onset is slow. Hyperglycemia is usually caused by stress, excessive carbohydrates, or missed insulin injections. If the symptoms occur, a doctor or school nurse should be called immediately and the parents notified. The student should be kept lying down and warm until medical help arrives.

2. *hypoglycemia* (also known as *diabetic shock*) – a serious condition, though less serious than hyperglycemia, resulting from too much insulin in the body which can result in convulsions or loss of consciousness. Symptoms may include dizziness, sweating, headaches, blurred vision, facial pallor, hunger, weakness, fainting, trembling, heavy heart beat, drowsiness, and confused thinking. Onset is rapid. Hypoglycemia is caused by too much physical activity, an overdose of insulin or insufficient eating. If symptoms occur, the student should be given a fruit drink or a drink with high sugar content, and the symptoms should subside within 10 to 15 minutes. The parents should be notified immediately after the incident. If the student convulses or becomes unconscious due to diabetic shock, do not give the student any food or liquid. Call the school nurse or doctor immediately.

Important Facts about Students with Juvenile Diabetes

- This disorder requires a great deal of personal involvement from the student. There are four factors which continually have to be dealt with: 1) blood glucose testing, 2) insulin therapy (usually by injection), 3) meal planning, and 4) exercise. These must be done on a rigid schedule or the health of the student can become compromised.

- People with diabetes tend to be more aware and involved with the maintenance of their health than any other medical disorder group.

- The student is the best manager of the disorder.

- Every student reacts to hyperglycemia and hypoglycemia differently and usually knows their particular symptoms.

- The student may have to be excused from class or classwork to take periodic blood glucose tests or to administer insulin shots.

- Students with diabetes must drink large amounts of water and consequently will need to use the bathroom more frequently.

- Some students with diabetes may not need to give themselves insulin shots because they wear an insulin pump. The teacher and classmates should be notified of the pump so caution can be exercised to avoid situations that may disrupt proper use of the device.

Suggestions for Working with a Student with Juvenile Diabetes

- Provide the student with a private location to test glucose levels and administer insulin injections. The bathroom is not a good option.

- Note the times the student is required to test glucose levels and administer insulin injections and remind the student when necessary.

- Be aware of the foods the student may not eat.

- Learn the student's particular hyperglycemic and hypoglycemic symptoms.

- Maintain an awareness of the student's appearance and activity.

- Expect to be asked to keep a bottle of fruit drink in your desk in case of an incidence of hypoglycemia.

- Allow the student to exercise at appropriate times and places.

Students with Epilepsy

Definition

Epilepsy is a disruption in the movement of electrical impulses through normal brain passages, which results in two degrees of seizures:

1. *tonic clonic* (previously called *gran mal*) – a type of seizure caused by large and uncontrolled amounts of electrical

energy in the brain resulting in symptoms that may last for several minutes and include loss of consciousness, convulsions, salivation, yelling, jerky movements, loss of bladder control and collapse, possibly followed by feelings of drowsiness, difficulty breathing, loss of color or inability to remember what happened; and

2. *absence seizures* (previously called *petit mal*) – a less severe type of seizure lasting 5 to 30 seconds and caused by smaller amounts of uncontrolled electrical energy in the brain, resulting in symptoms that may occur several times a day, which include staring or smiling (appearance of day-dreaming), droopy head, jerky movements, twitching arms and shoulders, rolling eyes or no reaction to dropping an object.

Important Facts about Students with Epilepsy

- People experiencing tonic clonic seizures are not at risk of swallowing their tongue.

- Some students experience a sensation called an "aura" which tells them when a seizure is coming.

Suggestions for Working with a Student with Epilepsy

- With the parents, school nurse and the student prepare a procedure for when a seizure occurs.

- If a student takes anti-seizure medication, ensure daily that it is being taken as prescribed.

- If a student experiences auras, plan a procedure and a safe place for the student to lie down, if one should occur.

- Watching a tonic clonic seizure can be very frightening. Inform the class about what to expect if the student has a seizure. Assign responsibilities to the class members, such as informing the office, moving furniture out of the way or going for the nurse.

- In case of a tonic clonic seizure, if possible:
  1. gently ease the person to the ground or to floor pillows;
  2. check for medical identification (this should be known in advance);

3. protect the student from nearby hazards;
4. remove the student's eyeglasses and loosen tight neckwear;
5. place a jacket or pillow under the student's head; and
6. turn the student on his side to clear airways.

Do not:

1. place anything in the student's mouth, particularly your fingers;
2. try to hold the student's tongue;
3. try to restrain the student;
4. try to give the student liquids during or immediately after the seizure; or
5. try to give the student medication during or immediately after the seizure.

Call for help if:

1. the seizure lasts for more than five minutes;
2. the seizure is followed by a second seizure;
3. the student is having difficulty breathing;
4. the student is injured, pregnant or diabetic;
5. the student requests it; or
6. the student was not previously known to be epileptic.

When the seizure ends, allow the student to rest and reassure the student and the class that everything is all right.

• Have the student keep a change of clothing on hand, as sometimes the student has a need for it.

• In case of an absence seizure, only be aware that the seizure has occurred and assure the student that everything is all right.

Students with Cystic Fibrosis

Definition

Cystic fibrosis is a progressive disorder characterized by damage to the lungs, abnormal mucus production and poor absorption of protein and fat. Damage to the lungs results in an inadequate supply of oxygen and eventual heart damage caused by lack of oxygen.

Important Facts about Students with Cystic Fibrosis

- Students with cystic fibrosis are subject to lung infections, pneumonia and collapsed lungs.

- Students with cystic fibrosis may require physical therapy, perhaps daily, to loosen the mucus secretions in the lungs.

- Associated digestive problems require such students to take vitamin and enzyme supplements and antibiotics to fight off frequent infections.

- Those afflicted with cystic fibrosis usually die by the age of twenty.

Characteristics of Students with Cystic Fibrosis

- Lack energy.

- May be in pain or discomfort.

- May have frequent and lengthy absences from school.

Suggestions for Working with a Student with Cystic Fibrosis

- Allow student to refrain, whenever necessary, from participating in an activity.

- Maintain an area where the student can lie down and rest.

- Maintain an awareness of how the student is doing when in your classroom.

- Prepare lessons that can be taken home or to the hospital during long absences.

Students with Cancer or Leukemia

Definition

Cancer is a condition in which a cell or group of cells escape the controls that regulate their growth and begin to spread, disrupting the body's normal functions.

Leukemia is a cancer in which abnormal blood cells accumulate in the blood, bone marrow and lymphatic tissues.

Important Facts about
Students with Cancer or Leukemia

- The severity of the condition and the ability to participate in class activities vary with the individual.

- Mortality rates due to cancer are decreasing as science and medicine advance. In 1965 the survival rate for people with cancer and leukemia was 4 percent. In 1995 it was about 72 percent.

- A student with cancer or leukemia will probably undergo therapy and treatment during school time necessitating frequent absences.

- Chemotherapy treatments lower the white blood cell count and make patients more prone to infections and other illnesses.

- Chemotherapy often causes hair loss. Students with hair loss are often subject to teasing from their classmates.

- Both cancer and chemotherapy can affect the central nervous system causing potential learning disabilities.

Characteristics of Students with Cancer or Leukemia

- May develop some learning disabilities if receiving cranial radiation.

- May display fatigue, weakness and low grade fever.

- May become easily bruised or bleed.

- May be in pain.

- May express anger or show depression because of condition.

Suggestions for Working with a
Student with Cancer or Leukemia

- Determine with the parents and the student whether the class should be told of the student's medical condition. If so, determine how the class should be told.

- Allow the student to take periodic rests. Maintain an area where the student can lie down.

- Encourage the class to include the student in all activities.

- Do not allow student to be teased.

184

- Allow the student to express feelings of anger and depression. However, the student should not be allowed to take out feelings on classmates.

- During sustained absences encourage the student's classmates to maintain relationships with the student by encouraging them to send notes and cards.

- During sustained absences maintain a relationship with the student by calling, visiting and staying informed of the student's treatment and progress.

- Be available to listen to the student's concerns and fears.

Students with HIV or AIDS

Definition

Human immunodeficiency virus (HIV) is a viral disease that breaks down the body's immune system making it vulnerable to invasion of other viruses.

Acquired immune deficiency syndrome (AIDS) is the final stage of HIV.

Important Facts about Students with HIV or AIDS

- HIV has three stages:
  1. *asymptomatic* – no symptoms of disease are present,
  2. *minor symptoms* – fever and fatigue, and
  3. *Acquired Immunodeficiency Disease* – one or more opportunistic infections and a T4 count below 200.

- Students born with HIV may not develop symptoms until they are two to five years old.

- Unlike other diseases, AIDS has legal protection for its confidentiality. Families need not disclose to the school that their child has AIDS. If the family chooses to disclose their child's condition to the school, the school must not divulge the information to anyone else without parental consent.

- AIDS usually ends in death. People do not die from AIDS but from AIDS-related illnesses.

- AIDS is contagious and is thought to be passed only through blood and some other bodily secretions. At present, there is no evidence that AIDS is passed through kissing, shaking hands, coughing, sneezing, swimming in a pool or being in proximity of an infected individual.

- AIDS carries a social stigma not found with any other disease. There is a strong tendency among many people to ostracize or persecute people who have AIDS.

- Children with AIDS are guaranteed a public education and are considered to be handicapped. However, should the child present a danger to others, (i.e., having open sores or a penchant for biting) the child may be excluded from the regular classroom as a health risk.

- Frequently changing laws and court decisions affect the way schools serve students with AIDS. Schools should periodically bring their staff up-to-date on the latest policies, especially when a student with AIDS is about to enroll.

Characteristics of Students with HIV or AIDS

- May lack energy and suffer from fatigue.

- May experience pain.

- May experience chronic diarrhea, reoccurring vaginal yeast infections and swollen glands.

- May have frequent illnesses and infections.

- May have frequent absences.

Suggestions for Working with a Student with HIV or AIDS

- Provide a great deal of moral support because the student may be ostracized by much of the community.

- Show compassion for the student and teach the classmates to do the same.

- Employ universal precautions to prevent the spread of HIV.

- Teach the class the truths and the myths of AIDS. Teach appropriate life procedures for preventing the spread of AIDS.

- Expect the student to develop diverse and frequent illnesses.

- When necessary, prepare lessons that can be done at home or in the hospital.

- During long absences keep the student connected to the class by exchanging notes, audio and video tapes, phone calls and visits.

- Because of some of the uncertainties that remain concerning AIDS, it is difficult to demand that a teacher fully support the inclusion of a student with AIDS in the classroom. Regardless of your past assumptions, you should be sympathetic and professional.

- Because of certain strong opinions expressed at home, it may be difficult to demand that the students fully support the inclusion of a child with AIDS. The teacher must at least protect the student from scorn and derision.

Students with Sickle Cell Anemia

Definition

Sickle cell anemia is an inherited chronic disease in which the red blood cells,which are normally disc shaped, become crescent shaped causing them to function abnormally so that they form blood clots and cause pain. These episodes of pain are referred to as "sickle cell pain crises."

Important Facts about Students with Sickle Cell Anemia

- Sickle cell anemia is found most often in African Americans.

- Sickle cell anemia can be so painful that hospitalization is required and can become so serious that it is life threatening.

- Some students with sickle cell anemia have special dietary requirements.

Characteristics of Students with Sickle Cell Anemia

- Experience joint pain and bone pain.

- Often suffer from fatigue.

- May experience rapid heart beat.

- May experience ulcers on lower legs.

- Have delayed growth and late onset of puberty.

- May have adverse responses to heat and cold.

Suggestions for Working with a
Student with Sickle Cell Anemia

- Allow the student to drink fluids. Allow the student to keep a receptacle of water or juice.

- Be aware of the condition of the student, particularly regarding pain.

- Administer pain medication as soon as pain begins.

- Have a place where the student can go if pain becomes intense.

- Provide the student with physical contact and emotional support to help him through pain.

Students with Birth Defects

Definition

Congenital malformations (birth defects) are abnormalities that occur when the mother ingests or comes in contact with substances that harm the fetus or when the fetus becomes malformed for other reasons. The main causes of birth defects are:

1. *fetal alcohol syndrome / fetal alcohol effects (FAS / FAE)* – a condition resulting from the mother drinking excessive amounts of alcoholic beverages while pregnant. The physical effects on the child may include slow growth development; facial deformities, such as drooping eye lids, wide nose, flattened mid-face; seizures; cerebral palsy; microcephalia; congenital heart disease; and mild or moderate mental retardation. The behavioral and cognitive effects on the child may include acting-out behavior, language delays, attention deficits, easy overstimulation, propensity to test limits, poor peer relationships, difficulties with organization and difficulties with problem solving.

2. *prenatal substance abuse* – a condition resulting from the mother ingesting illegal drugs while pregnant. The effects on the child may include language delays, attention problems and a variety of physical problems. These problems may be exacerbated by the economic and environmental conditions of the mother.

188

3. *misused drugs* – a condition resulting from the mother ingesting while pregnant, a prescribed drug (such as thalidomide) for a medical purpose that inadvertently harms the fetus. The effects on the child are numerous and varied. They include mental retardation, missing limbs, heart problems, and deformed limbs and facial features.

4. *accidental birth defects* – an incomplete or improperly formed part of the body or a body system that develops before birth. The effects on the child are varied. Most common are cleft palate, club foot, discrepancy in length of arms or legs, congenital hip dislocation, scoliosis, missing limbs or missing digits.

Important Facts about Students with Birth Defects

- Children subjected to prenatal substance abuse can have many problems beginning at birth, as addictive substances in their blood stream can immediately cause painful withdrawals after birth.

- Not every child born to a mother who abused drugs will show problems.

- Students who have been born with accidental defects, particularly a cleft palate, are subject to teasing from their classmates.

- The legal establishment in some states wants to make prenatal substance abuse a criminal offense.

- The most difficult and most diverse set of problems from this group will be presented by the children with FAS/FAE. In each case the individual child's problems will be addressed in the multi-disciplinary staffing. In most cases more than one adult at a time will be involved in the schooling of the child. The classroom teacher should not have the entire responsibility.

Suggestions for Working with a Student with Birth Defects

- If the defect has not affected the student's intelligence, assign the student the same work as the rest of the class.

- If the defect has affected the student's intelligence and the student has mental retardation, follow the guidelines in Chapter VI – Students with Mental Retardation.

- Help and encourage the student to explain the birth defect to the other students, who may be inquisitive.

- Because students with birth defects are subject to teasing, the teacher should model good behavior and insist on tolerance from the rest of the class.

Students with Hemophilia

Definition

Hemophilia is a serious and potentially life-threatening condition in which the blood is unable to clot.

Important Facts about Students with Hemophilia

- Hemophilia is usually genetic and most often found in males.

- Genetic testing and medical intervention have been able to greatly reduce the incidence of hemophilia.

Characteristics of Students with Hemophilia

- Suffer from bruising and spontaneous bleeding.

- Suffer from bleeding into joints, which causes swelling and pain.

- Suffer from gastrointestinal tract and urinary tract hemorrhages.

- Suffer from prolonged bleeding from cuts.

Suggestions for Working with a Student with Hemophilia

- Be constantly aware of the state of the student and the activities in which he is engaged.

- Ask other students to immediately report to you any incident in which the student has injured himself. Also make sure students know not to rough house with this student.

- Make sure there are written directions in your room for procedures to take should the student start bleeding.

Students Who Hyperventilate

Definition

Hyperventilation is a condition most often caused by over-excitement, resulting in too much oxygen in the blood system.

Important Facts about Students Who Hyperventilate

- There is no need to alter any work or provide any services for a student who hyperventilates, other than to treat the incidents of hyperventilation.

- Incidents of hyperventilation can be controlled by the student by being aware of when he is breathing too hard.

Characteristics of Students Who Hyperventilate

- Breathe rapidly.

- Become flushed.

- Become dizzy.

- May faint or lose balance and fall down.

Suggestions for Working with a Student Who Hyperventilates

- Have the student lie face up Place an open paper lunch bag over the student's mouth. Have the student breathe in and out of the paper bag. As the student breathes the recycled air, the amount of oxygen in the blood stream will be reduced, and the student will be able to gain full consciousness and resume class-work.

- Report all incidents of hyperventilation to the parents and to the designated school authority.

Students Who Have Been Abused

Definition

Parental child abuse is sexual abuse, excessive physical or emotional abuse, or neglect that causes physical or emotional damage to a child.

191

Important Facts about Students Who Have Been Abused

• Laws about reporting child abuse differ from state to state and are often revised. Schools should keep their teachers current on the necessary procedures for reporting cases of child abuse and should establish their own appropriate procedure.

• Laws and enforcement of laws about physical child abuse are vague in reference to the amount of corporal punishment parents can give their children. Usually the parents are not charged with a criminal offense, unless they inflict serious harm to a child. Even in such cases the state may be reluctant to act against the parent because the prevailing philosophy among the states' family and children departments is to keep the child with the parents whenever possible.

• Parents who shake their babies violently may cause serious brain damage, known as shaken baby syndrome. For working with these children, see Chapter XI – Students with Traumatic Brain Injury.

• Verbal child abuse is not against the law.

• Children who have been subject to child abuse may have central nervous system damage or traumatic brain injury. Physical damage may cause the child to be shorter and thinner than average. Psychological damage may cause excessive withdrawal, aggression, inability to trust others, destructive behavior, school failure or alcohol and drug abuse.

• Child abuse is a difficult problem to diagnose and usually requires a bond of trust between the teacher and the student. The student may volunteer information, or the teacher may suspect an abusive situation and ask the child for information.

Characteristics of Students Who Have Been Abused

• Often have bruises, burns, bite marks or swelling on arms, legs or torso.

• Prefer to be alone.

• May be withdrawn and secretive.

• May be aggressive and engage in rough play with classmates.

- Seldom invite classmates to their homes.

- Shrink when an adult passes closely.

- Resist having the school inform the parents of their inappropriate behavior. May panic.

Suggestions for Working with a Student Who Has Been Abused

- If a student reports being the victim of abuse, always follow school procedure in reporting it to the proper person in the building.

- Do not try to minimize the problem or talk the student out of discussing it. If you are uncomfortable in the role of listener, take (do not send) the student to the school counselor or other adult in the building who can handle the situation.

- Do not take the problem on yourself by calling or visiting the parents to discuss what their child has reported to you.

- In reporting the incident of child abuse to the proper administrator or counselor, report only what you know, not what you suspect or surmise.

- If you witness child abuse in your school you must report it.

- Do not intervene in family problems beyond giving moral support to your student.

Students with Childhood Obesity

Definition

Childhood obesity is excessive accumulation of body fat. Obesity is present when total body fat is more than 25 percent for boys and 32 percent for girls.

Important Facts about Students with Childhood Obesity

- About 14 percent of students aged 6 to 19 are seriously overweight. This number has tripled in the last 20 years.

- Students who are obese run increased risks for coronary heart disease, type 2 diabetes, hypertension and stress on joints.

- Students who are obese often have low self-esteem and are subject to peer rejection.

* Students who are obese are 70 percent more likely to be obese as adults than students who are not obese.

Characteristic of Students Who Are Obese

* Less likely to engage in physical activity due to the amount of energy needed to move their bodies.

* Likely to be self-conscious about their inability to perform well during physical activities.

Suggestions for Working with a Student Who Is Obese

* Teach units on what good nutrition is and why it is important.

* Actively engage the class in discussions on good nutrition.

* Encourage projects in healthy eating and exercise. Have students chart food intake and exercise.

* Encourage your school to maintain a full physical education program and recess.

* Do not give junk food as rewards.

* Try to develop goals and guidelines for a student who needs to lose weight. Give support.

Other Medical and Health Impairments

The following medical and health impairments are some that a teacher is likely to see in the classroom and should have some information about but do not require differentiated responses from those previously discussed.

cardiovascular problems – problems caused by improper formation or damage to the heart, usually congenital or acquired as a result of rheumatic fever or rubella

lead poisoning – abnormal levels of lead in the body, often the result of eating paint chips from the walls of pre-1960s buildings, which causes slowed mental development and low IQ

nephritis – inflammation of the kidney, resulting in such symptoms as fatigue, high blood pressure, swelling of the feet and ankles, and, if left untreated, possible kidney failure

rheumatic fever – heart-damaging illness characterized by fever, skin rash, nose bleeds and joint and abdominal pain that most often occurs in children 6 to 15 years of age within five weeks of contracting strep throat or scarlet fever

severe burns – burns resulting in severe scarring and disfigurement, usually to the hands and face, and requiring prolonged medical and surgical procedures to repair

Glossary

acute – developing quickly with intense symptoms

amniotic band syndrome – a condition resulting from fibrous bands of the placenta restricting the growth of the fetus

asymptomatic – not showing any symptoms (see *latency stage*)

chronic – developing slowly, lasting long and often retuning

crack cocaine – a type of cocaine that has been treated to make it produce a greater euphoria

epipen – name for the Epinephrine auto injector used to treat severe allergic reactions

latency stage – a period when an infection is not causing any symptoms (see *asymptomatic*)

muscle atrophy – the wasting away of muscle tissue due to disease or disuse

opportunistic infection – an infection which will attack people with HIV

partial seizure – an epileptic seizure that affects only part of the brain

respiratory ventilation – a procedure for suctioning off mucus through a small tube

service dog – a dog that has been specially trained to assist those with health impairments

T4 immune cells – the blood cells that fight infections and are a major target of HIV

Reference Books

Brotherson, M. J., L. Goldfarb, J. A. Summers, and A. Turnbull. *Meeting the Challenge of Disability or Chronic Illness – A Family Guide*. Baltimore, MD: Brookes Publishing Company, 1986.

Web Sites

Center for Disease Control
www.cdc.gov

Web M.D.
www.webmd.com

Asthma and Allergy Foundation of America
www.aafa.org

The Food Allergy Network
www.allergysupport.org

Association of Cancer Online Resources
www.acor.org

Cancer Kids
www.cancerkids.org

National Childhood Cancer Foundation
www.nccf.org

American Diabetes Association
www.diabetes.org

Children with Diabetes
www.childrenwithdiabetes.org

Juvenile Diabetes Research Foundation
www.jdf.org

Epilepsy Foundation
www.efa.org

National Pediatric and Family HIV Resource Center
www.pedhivaids.org

American Sickle Cell Anemia Association
www.ascaa.org

Chapter XV

Students with Terminal Illnesses

- *Students Who Are Dying*
- *Death of a Student*

Students Who Are Dying

Important Facts about Students Who Are Dying

- To have a student whose death is imminent is one of the most difficult tasks a teacher can encounter. Although everyone is aware of the approaching death, the student is best served when viewed as going on like every other student in the class. The dying student, especially during a time of being depressed, may question why he is being made to do classwork, "What is the point of learning algebra when I'll soon be dead?" Perhaps the best answer is, "Because you are alive now and this is what live people do."

- There is a tendency to move away from and avoid getting too attached to a student who is dying. Though the teacher may not be able to control this tendency, he does need to be aware of it because the dying student will be aware of people emotionally distancing themselves and may feel people don't like her anymore.

- Most school districts and several organizations devoted to with specific illnesses offer information and counseling to help people cope with the imminent death of a school friend.

Suggestions for Working with a Student Who Is Dying

- Guard against moving away emotionally.

- If the class knows of the student's impending death, always be aware that the students are looking to the teacher to see how they should act with the dying student.

- Consider working with the school counselor or an outside counselor to help the class understand what is taking place and how to cope with it.

- Answer questions the class may have. Discuss concerns honestly and in terms they can understand.

- Alert the other students' parents of the situation so they can answer their children's questions and comments made at home.

- If the student has been hospitalized or is having a long stay at home, encourage the class to write letters, draw pictures and send photos and videos, if the parents feel it is appropriate. If possible, have the ill student send notes and pictures to the class.

- Realize that the student's quality of life is more important than the production of schoolwork.

- Give the student art and creative writing assignments which can be left for family, friends and classmates as a legacy.

The Death of a Student

Important Facts about the Death of a Student

- The death of a student is a tremendous loss that is difficult for classmates, particularly young ones, to understand. It is also extremely difficult for the teacher, who is thrust into the role of being the strength of the class at a time of personal loss and vulnerability.

- Children's understanding of death is different according to their age. A general overview of their understanding follows:

Age 5–6 -	think the dead person can return
	may think they are responsible for the death
	may connect unrelated events to the death
	need to be assured that it is OK to cry
Age 6–9 -	may think the dead person can return
	may think they are responsible for the death
	fear that people close to them will die
	fear that death may be contagious
Age 9–12 -	have a better grasp of the finality of death
Age 12+ -	need to express feelings about death
	need to grieve in their peer group

- Some schools assume the teacher wants a grief counselor in the room if there has been a student death.

- It is all right for students and teachers to cry in class when grieving for a lost student.

- Many children have no experience with death and do not know what to do or how to act. The teacher becomes the model of appropriate behavior.

- The children may ask to do some artwork or writing in honor of

199

the student who has died. They may request that these works be given to the student's family.

Suggestions for Working with the Class after the Death of a Student

- In spite of your own grief, try to be with the class at this time.

- Cry in front of the class if you feel the need but do not break down completely. This would lead the children to feel that they need to take care of you at a time when they are particularly fragile. If you feel you are going to break down, ask a colleague to cover your class until such time as you can regain control.

- If desired, request that a counselor come to the room to give support. Allow the students to make comments freely and ask questions. Give answers honestly.

- Do not feel you are obligated to have a counselor in your room. If you prefer to be the only adult in the room with the class, request a counselor not be sent. Although a counselor knows more about grief than you do, you know more about your students.

- Discontinue regular classwork and assign appropriate activities to help the students grieve.

- Allow individual students to leave the room with other adults if they want to have a private talk or be away from the other students.

- Some students may voice unkind comments about the deceased student. Usually this is just their way of handling their grief and should not be taken seriously nor should the student be reprimanded at that time.

- Notify all parents of the death and their children's reactions.

- Ask the student's family if they wish to have classmates at the service, burial or after-burial visitation. Tell the students the family's wishes and ask the class to honor them. Unless otherwise requested, go to pay your respects to the family.

- If the student's classmates are attending the service, tell them how to dress, what to expect, and what to say and do. Ask several parents to attend with their children.

- If the students decide to do something in honor of the deceased student, such as paint a mural, or plant a tree, invite the student's family to attend. It will be meaningful if the family is given a collection of writings, poems or pictures from the class.

- Watch for individual class members who seem to be having difficulty resolving the death. Notify the children's parents and the school counselor.

- Be aware of your own feelings. Talk to someone, particularly a colleague who shares your knowledge of the deceased child.

Reference Books

Cassini, Kathleen, and Jacqueline Rogers. *Death and the Classroom.* Cincinnati, OH: Griefwork of Cincinnati, 1990.

Fitzgerald, Helen. *The Grieving Child—A Parent's Guide, A Fireside Book.* New York, NY: Simon and Schuster, 1992.

Shapiro, Ester R. *Grief as a Family Process.* New York, NY: The Guilford Press, 1994.

Webb, Nancy Boyd, ed. *Helping Bereaved Children.* New York, NY: The Guilford Press, 1993.

Web Sites

Beyond Indigo
www.beyondindigo.com

Bereaved Families On Line
www.bereaved families.net

Index